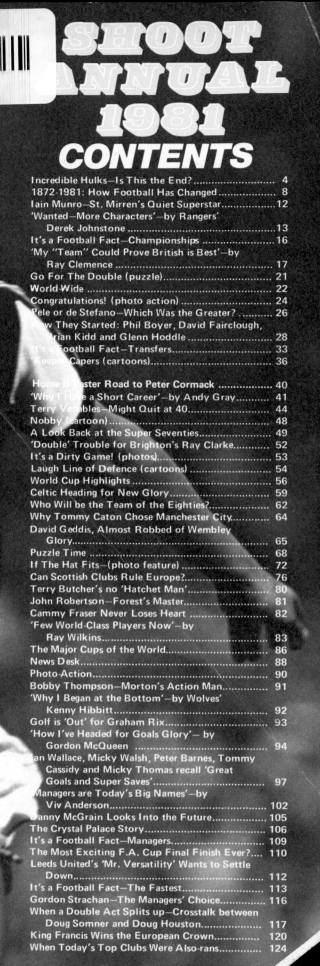

SHOOT ANNUAL 1981

CONTENTS

© IPC Magazines Ltd 1980
SBN 85037-580-0

Malcolm Macdonald, a "classic" striker (top left); Tommy Lawton (above), arguably the best England striker ever.

'INCREDIBLE HULKS' Is this the end?

A SK the average football fan anywhere in the world for his idea of a typical British international striker and he will paint a vivid picture of a cross between the Incredible Hulk and the Six Million Dollar Man.

His vision will be tall, with a strong honest face set beween brawny shoulders at least two coat hangers wide.

His trunk will be as wide as the average household door leading from the dining room to the kitchen, and his legs will be long and muscular, capable of eating-up distance with the tireless mobility of a marathon runner.

He will be acclaimed for his deadly shooting and heading power.

He will be scrupulously honest, fair, sporting and an ambassador for the game whenever he pulls on a shirt for his country even though his size is guaranteed to intimidate the majority of foreign defences.

They rely on strength and infinite courage, allied to more skill than they are ever given credit for. They are physical and brave.

Their job has been to harrass, bustle and bulldoze a path through defences;

to take the weight off the lighter forwards snapping at their shoulders, and to cause general mayhem in the opposing penalty-area in their quest for goals.

Tommy Lawton looked the part when he terrorised defences for England from the 1930s to the 1950s. He was six feet tall, straight and long, well slicked hair parted to the left of centre. He was the hero of most schoolboys of his era.

Malcolm Macdonald was a more recent version of this archtypal England centre-forward, a striker in the classic sense.

"Supermac" led the attack for Newcastle United, Arsenal and England before a knee injury forced him into premature retirement in the 1978-79 season with the flourish of one of those old-fashioned warriors into battle ahead of his troops. He was fast, powerful, brave, dangerous in the air and lethal with the ball on his left foot.

He scored goals in the grand manner. It was not "Supermac's" style to nick goals from one or two metres out. Goalkeepers twitched in nervous anticipation of a thunderbolt when he was within 30 yards of their netting.

Now there are growing signs that British football managers are looking for a more subtle way of breaking down international defences, a more delicate instrument to achieve the same effect of scoring more goals than the opposition.

England's manager Ron Greenwood could be poised to abandon the traditional style of centre-forward which has served England so well over the years.

The England manager hints that he

is by no means committed to employing a blunt instrument in the number nine shirt. He suggests that England could field a side without a recognised centre-forward.

"Do you need a centre-forward?" argues Greenwood. "I'm not sure you do. I shook a few people when I managed West Ham by using Budgie Byrne as a striker. He had no height and not much weight, but he was mighty effective. Nothing like your traditional type of centre-forward."

Greenwood believes in loyalty. He persevered with Bob Latchford, a centre-forward cast from the same mould as Lawton and Macdonald, even though big Bob was out of touch at Goodison Park in Football League matches in the 1979-80 season.

But when the moment came for a change in England's line-up as they surged thrillingly to the finals of the European Championship in 1980, the England manager had no hesitation in selecting the smaller, faster Trevor Francis for the striker's role.

Greenwood still maintains that if a League club have a 6ft. 3ins. tall striker, weighing 15 stone, who scores goals regularly, he would be a certainty for selection to Greenwood's squad.

Size is unimportant if the ability is there, claims Greenwood. Yet the England boss is not alone among international football chiefs in believing

Trevor Francis (right) is smaller and faster than the average striker.

4

that central attackers will have to become more mobile in the 1980s. Defences are becoming more sophisticated requiring attacks to become more subtle. The theory is that it is better to "ghost" into shooting positions by employing attackers moving from deep positions rather than thrust an obvious heavyweight attacker into the fray which the opposing defence can snuff out.

It was no surprise to Greenwood that Kevin Keegan should score both England's winning goals against the Republic of Ireland, at Wembley, in February 1980. Keegan was in the programme as a midfield player. He spent much of his time patrolling the centre of the famous arena but whenever the opportunity arose he was scuttling between the Republic's defensive ranks.

Tony Woodcock IS an official striker for England, yet he is hardly of the same physique as many of his predecessors chosen for his country. Woodcock relies on pace and shrewd positioning, allied to a nose for goals.

Garry Birtles is another "hare" for defences to chase. He looks a pale, slip of a player in a Nottingham Forest shirt but Brian Clough and Peter Taylor had no hesitation in promoting him quickly to first team football after signing him for Forest from a non-league club.

Greenwood carried on the good work by elevating Birtles to his young England side and there are firm hopes he will graduate to England's attack on a regular basis by the 1982 World Cup Finals.

There was a time when a player would not have the audacity to call himself a striker if he was less than six feet tall.

Terry Connor, Leeds United's exciting young black striker, is dwarfed when he comes into contact against big central defenders, but Connor is never overawed and is tipped to win representative honours.

Manchester United have used Lou Macari (below) as a striker.

Gary Birtles is a "hare" for defences to chase. He could become England's striker.

Many professionals are convinced that big strikers are unnecessary.

"Manchester United have proved they can do without the traditional centre-forward by using Steve Coppell and Lou Macari up-front whenever Joe Jordan is injured," observes Joe Gallagher, Birmingham City's tough Scottish defender.

"Steve and Lou are both small and it suited United to use them in attack in the 1979-80 season. I remember when Birmingham played Watford, it took some time for myself and the rest of our defence to adjust to Watford not using a recognised centre-forward, relying instead on two men on each flank.

"On the other hand, a fit Joe Jordan leading the Manchester United attack is a formidable opponent, and I think a team can be effective up-front by adopting the style that suits them best with the players available."

Bristol City's John Shaw says the old-style battering ram centre-forward is fast fading in the First Division.

"But having said that there is still room in some teams for the spearhead leaders such as Bob Latchford, Joe Royle and Andy Gray. In the Second, Third and Fourth Division where there is less skill, more teams rely on big fellows up front.

"Liverpool use Dalglish and Johnson as decoys, moving away to leave space for such as Ray Kennedy or Terry McDermott."

The traditional style of striker is not "necessary", says John Craggs, Middlebrough's long-serving full-back.

"I remember playing against Everton, and Bob Latchford. They relied on aiming long balls into our penalty area. It gave our defence a lot of work—but they would have put much more pressure on us if they had had the players who could have got behind our defenders.

"However, it is a fact that if a team continually pumps high balls into the opposing penalty-area, a certain percentage of these will be won in the air by a big, spearhead-type of centre-forward—and from his flicks and knockdowns, his team-mates may be able to create goal chances.

"In my opinion, the most difficult of the traditional, big, robust centre-forwards to mark is Joe Royle. When Joe is getting the service he can create problems for defenders throughout the 90 minutes."

Managerial opinion suggests that the 1980's could produce fewer big strikers.

So perhaps we should pay tribute to a dying breed of superstars who won the hearts of the fans with their deeds.

Lawton, who played 23 times for England, was as good in the air as most strikers are on the ground. His astonishing spring took him into regions which most men are happy to leave to insects and birds. Playing against Charlton once, their former goalkeeper Sam Bartram tells the story of the day Lawton leapt high in Charlton's penalty area and shouted: "Top left hand corner, Barty." and that's where the ball went!

Stan Mortensen, shorter and stockier than Lawton, scored four goals in England's 10—0 humiliation of Portugal in 1947, his first full international. Lawton also scored four goals in that game. The England forward line that day made glorious reading: Matthews, Mortensen, Lawton, Mannion, Finney.

Morty's last and 25th appearance for England was at Wembley in 1953. Hungary 6, England 3. .... and Mortensen scored that day too.

Jackie Milburn, capped 13 times by England in days when there were fewer international games, was comic-hero material. His initials were J.E.T. No letters were strung together more aptly. Milburn had the burning pace of an Olympic sprinter. His robust, tearaway style brought him 196 goals for Newcastle between the end of the War and 1957.

Bolton's Nat Lofthouse was another battering-ram. The former Wales and Arsenal goalkeeper Jack Kelsey considered Nat the best centre-forward he played against. Lofthouse was murder for goalkeepers at a time when shoulder-charging was allowed.

Lofthouse's winning goal for England against Austria in the Prater Stadium in 1952 earned him the title of "Lion of Vienna". Finney slipped him a pass in the middle of the pitch and Lofthouse surged forward on the longest run of his life before angling the ball coolly past Musil.

John Charles was another collosus. He is considered by many observers to be the best player Wales have produced. He stood 6ft 2ins tall and weighed 14 stone, yet controlled a football with the dexterity of a lightweight winger. He was christened the "Gentle Giant" in the colours of Leeds United twice, Juventus, Roma and Cardiff.

Tommy Taylor's flame flickered briefly before it was extinguished in the Manchester United air disaster at Munich in 1957. The high-scoring number nine made 19 England appearances before he perished with some of the "Busby Babes".

Geoff Hurst, a carbon copy of "Roy of the Rovers", was a wing-half at West Ham before their manager Ron Greenwood converted him to a striker with stunning effect.

He went on to make 49 England appearances but will always be remembered for becoming the first player to score a hat-trick in a World Cup Final.

Jimmy Greaves, Kevin Keegan and Kenny Dalglish have relied on mobility, speed and sharp-shooting for their goals rather than brawn.

But it will be a long time before Britain buries its reputation for producing king-sized strikers who set the terraces alight with their goal-scoring talents and courage.

GERRY GOW
Bristol City

6

ANDY KING
Everton

7

1872-1981 How football has changed!

NO sport has seen more changes over the years than Soccer, changes that have helped to make it the greatest game not only in Britain but throughout the world.

Take the Football League for example. Did you know, for instance, that when the formation of a league was introduced in 1888, three years after professionalism was legalised by the F.A., only twelve clubs accepted the invitation. They were Preston North End, Aston Villa, Wolves, Blackburn, Bolton, West Bromwich Albion, Accrington Stanley, Everton, Burnley, Derby County, Notts County and Stoke. Not a Southern club among them you'll notice!

Preston North End were Champions in the first two seasons of the League and Stoke finished bottom on each occasion. In 1891, however, the League was extended to 14 clubs and in 1892 the number was doubled with the formation of a Second Division—16 clubs in the First and 12 in the Second. A year later Division Two was increased to 15 clubs with the entry of Arsenal and Liverpool, and to 20 clubs in each section in 1905. Thus it remained until 1919 when both sections were increased to 22.

Other clubs began to clamour for inclusion and in 1920 the Third Division was formed. The League grew even bigger in 1921 when it was split into two sections, South and North, with 22 members in each, only the leaders of each section were promoted. In 1949 the two Thirds were increased to 24 clubs and in 1958 the top 12 clubs in each section became the Third Division and the remaining 24 formed the new Fourth Division. So in the space of 65 years the Football League had increased from 12 to 92 members.

During that time, of course, several clubs have fallen by the wayside, mainly due to financial problems, but there has never been any shortage of applications from other clubs for membership of the greatest League in the football world.

Before the start of the 1973-74 season the League instituted another change in the promotion and relegation laws that was to give a much needed fillip to end of the season struggles in all four Divisions. It was revolutionary but few would deny that it has proved successful. Instead of the old system of two up and two down the League decided that it should be three clubs down from Division One and three up from Division Two; three from Division Two into the Third and replaced by the top three in the Third.

Some years earlier, when the two Third Division (South and North) came into being, it was decided that FOUR clubs should be relegated from Third to Fourth, with promotion for the top four in the lowest section. How very different from the days of the 1890's when there was no automatic promotion and relegation between the top and bottom clubs in the *two* divisions. The last three clubs in the First and the top three in the Second contested a series of "Test" matches, the winners of which decided which two should be promoted or relegated. The system was soon dropped. however. There is nothing really to compare with the Football League for drama, thrills and suspense. The drama extends over a period of nine months as the clubs battle it out for the Championship, promotion and the grim suspense of those fighting against relegation. Perhaps that is why most clubs and players regard the winning of the Championship as far greater than victory in the Cup Final.

The Championship demands sustained success over 42 matches, but it takes only seven victories to win the Cup. Yet, of course, the F.A. Cup attracts even greater interest among the fans than the League Championship. It wasn't always so . . . . . .

C. W. Alcock

Spurs v. Sheffield United at Crystal Palace . . . 1901 F.A. Cup Final.

The Football Association Challenge Cup, to give it its full title, was instituted way back in 1871, the brainchild of Mr. C.W. Alcock, secretary of the Surrey County Cricket Club, who had taken over a similar position with the Football Association. There was little organised competition between the few amateur clubs in those days and such a competition he felt would help to increase the competitive nature of the game. He could never have realised that his idea was to produce such far reaching proportions.

Fifteen teams entered for the first Cup competition, all from the South except Queen's Park, Glasgow, who were excused entry until the Semi-Finals because of the long travelling that was involved. The first Final was played at the Oval between Wanderers and the Royal Engineers, before a crowd of less than 2,000. Wanderers were given a walk-over into the Final because their Semi Final with Queen's Park was drawn and the Scots could not afford to travel to London for the replay! Can you imagine that happening today? Or a crowd of 2,000 to watch a Final played on a cricket pitch? There wasn't even a trophy to present to the winners — it hadn't been delivered from the makers!

By 1875 the lure of the Cup attracted 32 entries, although the greater majority of them were from the South, and all amateurs, of course. From then on more and more clubs joined the Cup race, including Nottingham Forest. Yes, it's true, but remember they were then an amateur side. The F.A. continued to refuse entry to any club who paid their players — even expenses — but in 1883 they had to admit, reluctantly, that if the Cup competition was to become "nationwide" the growing power of the Northern clubs had to be accepted.

So in 1884, the first 100 entries was reached. Blackburn Rovers became the first professional side to win the trophy. Rovers retained the Cup the following year and on each occasion they beat Queen's Park, Glasgow, the last amateur side to reach the Final.

Disastrous

It soon became apparent that the Oval, with a capacity of little more than 20,000 was no longer big enough for the Final. In 1893 the big match was played at Fallowfield, an athletics ground at Manchester. It proved disastrous, so Everton's Goodison Park was given the next Final. But in 1895 the venue was switched to Crystal Palace and it was there that the Cup Final drew its first 100,000 gate in 1901. Twenty two years later Bolton and West Ham met in the First Final at Wembley. Today even Wembley Stadium is not big enough to accommodate the multitude of fans wanting to watch the Final, but it will have to suffice until the F.A. decide to build a new super-stadium . . . .

So much for the Football League and the F.A. Cup, but today there is yet another competition that has captured the imagination of the fans and brought new honours to clubs and players alike, the Football League Cup. This new trophy competition was instituted by the Football League in 1960, all the ties to be played in mid-week under floodlights. To many of the smaller clubs it seemed a godsend, financially in particular. Yet quite a number of the bigger clubs were far from ecstatic. They felt the season's programme was more than sufficient. They objected to more midweek matches. Eventually most of them decided to enter but Arsenal, Spurs, Sheffield Wednesday, West Brom and Wolves decided to sit it out on the sidelines.

That first League Cup competition eventually got under way but as the season progressed it was obvious there were problems. According to the rules of the competition the Semi-Finals were to be decided over home and away legs, so was the Final. After a long drawn-out contest, due mainly to replays in so many of the fixtures, Aston Villa and Rotherham reached the Final, which had to be delayed until the early weeks of the following season. Villa won 3—2.

Not until 1965 did the first of the disinterested clubs, West Bromwich Albion, decide to enter for the League trophy. They celebrated their debut by beating West Ham 5—3 in the two leg Final. The next season Arsenal, Spurs, Sheffield Wednesday and Wolves felt it was time they, too, joined the band wagon, especially when it was announced that in the future the League Cup winners would earn entry to the next season's European Fairs Cup competition (now, if course, the UEFA Cup).

So the Football League Cup became accepted throughout the English clubs. Today the Final attracts a capacity crowd at Wembley and puts thousands of pounds into the coffers of the Finalists.

Nottingham Forest after their 1979 League Cup success.

STEVE COPPELL
Man. Utd.
and England

10

KEVIN REEVES
Norwich City

The title of 'Quiet Superstar' sits fairly and firmly on St. Mirren's multi-talented left-back Iain Munro.

Not that long ago it looked as though he was going to become one of football's forgotten men heading for the scrapheap long before his time. He was languishing in the Rangers reserves and his future looked bleak.

He recalls: "I had signed for Rangers from Hibs in a swop deal that took Ally Scott and Graeme Fyfe to Hibs. I thought it really was the start of something good.

"Rangers are a glamour club constantly in the hunt for honours and I was eager to get in on the action. But it didn't turn out that way. For some

and just over a year ago Stoke City were reported to have been unsuccessful in a £300,000 bid for the player. That's inflation for you!

Munro's consistently superb displays in the Paisley rearguard won him rave notices and it wasn't long before Scotland team manager Jock Stein was taking his seat in the Love Street stand to watch the player in action.

Actually, Stein already knew all about Munro's capabilities. He had been an admirer for some time and it seemed certain that the player might have landed at Parkhead if he hadn't gone to Ibrox first.

Munro made his international debut

IAIN MUNRO -THE "QUIET SUPERSTAR"

reason or another, my face just did not fit. My first team appearances were few and far between."

Ironically Munro's career was given the kiss of life by a former Ranger Alex Ferguson, the current Aberdeen manager. Four years ago he was in charge of the up-and-coming St. Mirren side and he desperately needed experience in his ranks to nurse along players such as Frank McGarvey and Tony Fitzpatrick, who have since moved on, of course.

Ferguson saw Munro as that man and for an almost unbelievable £25,000 he coaxed Rangers into parting with him. At once Munro's career took off

against the world champions Argentina in a Challenge Match at Hampden and he says: "What a fabulous experience. I had represented my country at other levels such as schools and youths, but to get into the big team was something else altogether.

"Believe me, it is a great feeling to play for your country. I was really proud. I wasn't afraid of making my debut against Argentina. Why should I have been?

"I had always believed in my own ability. I don't want to sound big-headed, but I knew what I could do and I was determined to show it to everyone. It took me a while to get started, but once I got into my stride I enjoyed myself.

"Scotland lost 3-1 unfortunately, but The Press gave me some nice write-ups although I knew I could still do a lot better. Still, it was a good experience and one I want to continue obviously."

The clever and articulate Munro is a manager's dream. He is a dedicated team man, a good trainer and he never attracts any bad publicity off the field.

Munro, who, incidentally, started his career at St. Mirren alongside Gordon McQueen before going on to Hibs, is enjoying his best spell in soccer and St. Mirren fans—and all neutral fans, too—are thankful that he still has a lot to offer before the sad day when he decides to hang up his boots.

Alex Ferguson (left) signed Iain Munro (far left) from Rangers when he was manager of St. Mirren.

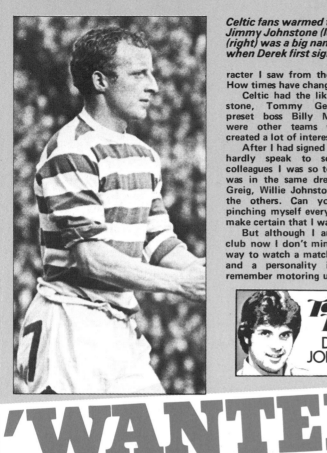

Celtic fans warmed to the tricks of Jimmy Johnstone (left). Colin Stein (right) was a big name at Rangers when Derek first signed for the club.

racter I saw from the Tannadice stand. How times have changed!

Celtic had the likes of Jimmy Johnstone, Tommy Gemmell and their preset boss Billy McNeill and there were other teams with players who created a lot of interest.

After I had signed for Rangers I could hardly speak to some of my new colleagues I was so tongue-tied. There I was in the same dressing room as Mr. Greig, Willie Johnston, Colin Stein and the others. Can you blame me for pinching myself every now and again to make certain that I wasn't dreaming?

But although I am with a glamour club now I don't mind going out of the way to watch a match if I have the time and a personality is playing. I can remember motoring up to Pittodrie with

Tartan Talk
DEREK JOHNSTONE

'WANTED~
MORE CHARACTERS'

SOCCER fans find quite a lot to complain aobut these days and I certainly wouldn't deny them that right.

I go to a lot of supporters' functions on behalf of Rangers and I'm interested in listening to what the fans have to say. After all, they are the lifeblood of the game and without them you have nothing.

One topic that continually comes up in conversation is the supposed lack of REAL personalities in today's game. Some old-stagers say that the managers are becoming the stars and the players are being forgotten.

Certainly everyone knows all about Brian Clough, Malcolm Allison, Bob Paisley and the like so I suppose it is an interesting arguement. But I would hate to think that the days of the real characters, the crowd pleasers are over.

When I was a youngster I supported Dundee United and used to go along to Tannadice with a huge tangerine scarf round my neck. I was just like any other young fan and I couldn't see past my favourites, but I know I used to get an extra feeling of drama on the day of the match if a big-name player was in the opposition.

For instance, Rangers had Jim Baxter ———later to become a team-mate of mine at Ibrox———and he was always a popular figure. Fans would turn up in all conditions to see him in action with that wonderful left foot.

I don't want the gaffer, John Greig, to feel too old, but he was another cha-

a friend one night about eight years ago when Manchester United were due to play Aberdeen in a Challenge Match.

The man I wanted to see was George Best, one of the all-time greats so far as I am concerned. United were walloped 5-2 that evening, but I still got a thrill out of watching the Irishman in action. He did little things that had class stamped all over them, but, unfortunatly for him that night, he got little response from his team-mates.

I met him a couple of times after that and was always amazed about how quiet and shy he was. People who expected him to go crazy and whoop it up were always sadly disappointed.

Another favourite was the one and only Denis Law, Best's team-mate at Old Trafford for a while, of course. I think every Scottish kid idolised Law. He was a real demon in that penalty box with his lightning reflexes.

He had so much ability, didn't he? There wasn't an awful lot of him, but he wasn't frightened to get in there and mix it with the best of them. And what about his ability in the air? People say I'm fairly useful with my napper and I suppose I have knocked in a few in the past and I hope to continue in the future, but Law was something else altogether.

Law fired himself at the ball with all sorts of acrobatic leaps and goalkeepers must have demanded danger money before facing him.

Yes, I take the supporters' point when they demand to see more personalities. Don't we all? Possibly the youngsters of today are being overcoached too soon and this is stifling their natural ability. It's also feasible that there is too much pressure in big-time football today for players to take the chance and express pressure in big-time football today for players to take the chance and express their individualism.

Whatever the reason, it would be good to see more characters emerging in the next decade. I'm keeping my fingers crossed!

Derek Johnstone

DAVID O'LEARY
Arsenal

PETER WARD
Brighton

15

It's a Football Fact
League Championship

First three-time winners

The first club to win the Football League Championship three times in a row was Huddersfield Town 1923-24, 24-25 and 25-26. Their record was even more remarkable when considered in the light of the fact that when peace-time football had resumed in 1919 they were in the Second Division, heavily in debt, and considering a move to the ground of the old Leeds club which had just been forced out of existence. However, they decided to stay at Huddersfield and not only won promotion in 1920 but appeared in the Cup Final as well (losing 1-0 to Aston Villa). Their Championship-winning team included no less than 15 players who appeared in each of those three seasons. The mainstays of the side throughout this period were centre-half Tom Wilson and left half Billy Watson. They never dropped below 40 appearances apiece in each of those three glorious campaigns.

109 Goals in 196 Games

It is worth noting that Cliff Bastin has one of the most remarkable records among Championship-winning medallists. He not only collected five of these trophies but played in a total of no less than 196 Championship-winning games, scoring 109 goals. He was one of the hardest and most accurate shots in the game and in the 1932-33 Championship-winning campaign set up a First Division record by scoring 33 goals as a winger.

"Team of all the talents"

The record points-winning margin for a Football League Championship team is 11. Preston North End were that much ahead of their nearest rivals when they won the title in the League's initial season of 1888-89, and this record was subsequently equalled by Sunderland (1892-93), Aston Villa (1896-97), and Manchester United (1955-56). Preston's victory was convincing enough considering that they are still the only side to have been undefeated in a season of Football League matches. However, they played only 22 games, and probably the most convincing Championship win among this quartet of runaway victories was Sunderland's. Their side at that time were known as the "Team of all the Talents" and 1892-93 was the second successive campaign in which they carried off the League's blue riband, They scored 100 goals in only 30 games, a total not exceeded until after World War 1 when the season was extended to one of 42 games. The team was composed almost entirely of Scotsmen.

Robbed of "double"

If your favourite team gets off to a bad start in the season do not despair, but consider Sunderland's astonishing recovery after a disastrous start in 1912-13. The Roker Park club failed to win any of their first seven games, in which they collected only two points, but they went on to win the First Division Championship with a total of 54 points, which was a record number up to that time. They finished four points ahead of their nearest rivals, Aston Villa, whom they also met in that season's F. A. Cup

Final, being prevented from winning the "double" by an only goal.

Great Gunners

The only other club to win the Championship three seasons in succession was Arsenal in 1932-33, 33-34 and 34-35. Eleven players appeared in all three of these seasons, and most of them were household names like Cliff Bastin, Eddie Hapgood, Joe Hulme, Alex James and George Male.

Penalty took title

Another side to win the Championship after a poor start to the season was Chelsea in 1954-55, their Golden Jubilee year and the first in which they won the title. Chelsea won only three of their first nine games and even when they had reached the half-way mark in their campaign they were no higher than eighth position. This, however, was one of those remarkably even tussles in which no side really reigned supreme, and halfway through the season only four points separated the leaders (Wolves) from the club in 13th position. Chelsea really clinched the title that season on Easter Saturday when, before a crowd of over 75,000 at Stamford Bridge and many more locked out, they beat Wolves with the only goal scored from the penalty spot by Peter Sillett.

Ever presents

Throughout the history of the Football League only six players have appeared in *every* First Divison game during *two consecutive* Championship-winning seasons. The first to achieve this distinction were goalkeeper, Ted Doig, and right-back, Tom Porteous, of Sunderland, who each played in all 56 games when their side won the title in 1891-92 and 1892-93 i.e. 26 games in the first season and 30 in the second. The more recent instances are more remarkable because being ever-present in two consecutive Championship-winning seasons involves 84 games. Three of these players are among Liverpool's medal winners — Dick Forshaw 1921-22 and 1922-23 (He also won a medal with Everton in 1927-28), and more recently, goalkeeper Ray Clemence and full-back Phil Neal

in seasons 1975-76 and 1976-77. The other players making up this famous half-dozen is that tricky little Sheffield Wednesday winger, Mark Hooper, who was an ever-present when Wednesday carried off the title in 1928-29 and again

the following season. Those were the days!

Liverpool's Phil Neal (dark strip), an ever-present in two Championship seasons.

'MY "TEAM" COULD PROVE BRITISH IS BEST'

Ray Clemence
TALKING SOCCER

THE four Home nations should combine to form a British team for international competition! That cry is heard periodically from some sections in the British Isles, who maintain that such a team would be certain to enjoy more success than is individually achieved by the four separate countries.

It's also echoed by other nations, jealous of the fact that tradition has bestowed on Britain the right to four entries in every competition.

In my view the idea is completely impractical for many reasons. The main one is of the players' loyalty to their countries. The break from tradition, established over almost a hundred years, would damage their morale. It would take ages, if ever, to breed alliegance to a British team, made up of men from different cultures.

Foreign critics point out the unfairness of having four teams from two islands when a vast country like Russia, made up of several states, is entitled to field only one side.

But on that basis, a country such as the United States would be allowed 50 teams!

No, England, Northern Ireland, Scotland and Wales must continue as separate entities as far as football is concerned.

That isn't to say that occasionally they shouldn't combine forces, for some special

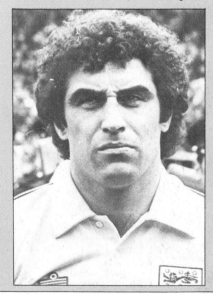

Peter Shilton . . . "doesn't possess a single weakness. He is extremely brave."

But then I've always believed in going in at the deep end!

Firstly I must decide on how "my" team would play, as that to a great extent governs the selection of players.

And what better than 4-4-2, the formation that has served Liverpool so well over the years!

For the goalkeeper's spot I have no hesitation in writing down the name of Peter Shilton, for the last few years my main rival for the England number one jersey.

Steve Coppell ... "has made the transition from Fourth Division football with Tranmere to the top flight."

Dave Watson (above) ... "whose style I know so well through having him in front of me for England." Phil Thompson (below right) ... "to fill the spot alongside Dave."

occasion, and play a representative side from South America, Africa, Asia or Europe.

There would be tremendous interest generated by a match between a British select eleven and one from a major soccer-playing group of countries.

But who would manage and pick Britain's team? His selection would probably be the biggest stumbling block of all: to find someone respected by all four nations and granted the power to build a representative side that would do justice to the tremendous amount of talent in British football.

For the purpose of this article I'm going to put my head on the chopping block and assemble my version of a combined team. I don't expect many readers to agree with me, but I guarantee it will spark off a lot of discussion in the pubs, clubs and schools.

For someone who has yet to start out on a managerial career, it's an ambitious step.

At one time, Peter was criticised for lack of concentration on the ground. If it was justified then, it certainly couldn't be supported now, as in my view he doesn't possess a single weakness. Not only is he faultless technically, he is also extremely brave—an essential quality in a 'keeper, who at times must dive unhesitatingly into a mass of kicking boots for the ball.

On the right of my back-four I'd place Sandy Jardine of Scotland and Rangers, whom I've admired while playing against him in games between the "Old Enemies" and also on TV.

He's impressive in defence, and can also add his weight to the attack when necessary.

In the centre of the back-four I deliberated between picking either Gordon McQueen or Dave Watson. At one time Gordon tended to allow his enthusiasm to cause him to go for goal too much instead of helping to guard his own net. But recently

box!

Alongside him I'd place his United team-mate Sammy McIlroy, who last season probably had his best-ever for for his club and country. Against England last year in Belfast, he was the only Northern Ireland player to continually present us with prolems.

There are so few Welsh players in our First Division only one qualifies for my team—Brian Flynn of Leeds United. What little Brian lacks in inches, he more than makes up for with heart.

He's a tireless worker, and his continual buzzing about the pitch forces opponents into errors and creates goal-chances for himself and his team-mates.

I make no apologies for choosing Ray Kennedy, of Liverpool and England, for the left-sided place in midfield. It wasn't until last season that Reds' fans and the Press generally appreciated how vital he is

he has concentrated more on his defensive duties, and so become a better player.

But Dave Watson, whose style I know so well through having him in front of me for England, just has the edge over Gordon.

My "team" would stand little chance if all the players were "Strangers", and unaccustomed to combining together. That's one of the reasons I choose Phil Thompson, my Liverpool and England team-mate, to fill the spot alongside Dave Watson.

The two of them compliment each other so well I'd have every confidence in them against the best attack in the world.

Problem Position

I gave a lot of thought to the left-back position, probably the one all managers have problems in filling at the moment.

Finally I plumped for Frank Gray, who has improved since his move from Leeds

Sammy McIlroy . . . "last season probably had his best-ever for club and country." Brian Flynn (right) . . . "what he lacks in inches, he more than makes up for with heart."

United to Nottingham Forest under manager Brian Clough and assistant Peter Taylor. Like Sandy Jardine, on the opposite side of the back-four, Frank can switch to an attacking role.

My first choice in midfield is Steve Coppell, of Manchester United and England, a great worker with abundant skill who has made the transition from Fourth Division football with Tranmere to the top flight.

Steve, apart from the ability to support the front-runners, can also score goals—mainly from close in. It's a joke amongst the England players that Steve's goals invariably come from within the six-yard

My third sub is Asa Hartford, of Everton, a very skilful and whole-hearted player for club and country who often doesn't get the credit he deserves.

Alongside him on the bench would be fellow Scot Kenny Burns, a key figure with Nottingham Forest.

As cover for Kenny and Kevin I'd go for Alan Curtis, now with Leeds, a lad who came to prominence with Swansea.

Well, there you have it—my team of All-Stars I'd back against any other select side in the World to prove that British is best!

Now I'll leave you to argue it out amongst yourselves!

See you in SHOOT—every week.

Ray Clemence

Kenny Dalglish (left), and Kevin Keegan (below)... "Kenny is a deadly finisher, and Kevin is now his equal."

in the Liverpool set-up when he was out injured for several games.

He is essential to give balance to any side fortunate enough to have him in its squad.

I like the look of my midfield. Every one of the four can carry out all the required duties, including scoring goals themselves as well as making them for others.

For my two front-runners I unhesitatingly write down the names of men I regard as supreme in not only Europe but the World. Kenny Dalglish and Kevin Keegan.

Kenny is a deadly finisher—and Kevin, since playing on the Continent with Hamberger SV, is now his equal.

Both can hold on to balls thrown up to them by the defence and midfield and by so doing allow other players to come up in support.

What an exciting thought—Kenny and Kevin teamed together against international opposition!

Every team needs substitutes who can be slotted in without weakening it. The five I've got in mind wouldn't let me down.

Firstly, Joe Corrigan of Manchester City, a great 'keeper whose bad luck is having Peter Shilton and myself around when otherwise he'd be first choice for England.

Secondly, Phil Neal, another of my Liverpool and England team-mates, who can play at either right or left back.

Go For The Double

Answers on Page 32

After you have completed the crossword in the normal way . . .

The letters in squares: 2, 6, 10, 13, 15, 17, 18, 28, 33, 35, 36, 45, 48, 50 and 52 can be made into the name of a very famous player.

The letters in the thick-edged squares can be made into the name of another famous English League Club.

Across

(1) Danny _____, captain of the Spurs 'double' winning team.
(8) Coventry City, The _____ Blues.
(9) Famous Wolves player, capped 105 times by England. (5 & 6)
(12) L—d— Road (Huddersfield Town). The omissions reversed.
(13) ———drie play at Broomfield Park.
(14) Alan——dd, Stoke City defender.
(15) Boo—hf—rr— Park (Hull City). More omissions reversed.
(17) Strong emotional impression
(19) WBA made an historic trip to this country in 1978.
(21) D——seldorf. West German League club.
(22) ———chester Unite—, The U's.
(23) Dynamo—, UEFA Cup Winners, 1976.
(26) B—n——r, Irish League club.
(27) "The —", nickname of Brentford F.C.
(29) ———mf—rd Bridge (Chelsea). The missing letters reversed.
(31) There's a famous one running through Manchester.
(32) ———a—fi—ld Stadium (Clyde). Chops from the missing letters.
(33) Nearby. As in "your — football club".
(34) Brian L——tle, Aston Villa striker.
(35) —Finney, Footballer of the Year.
1953/4 & 1956/7.
(36) Ground of Manchester City. (5 & 4)
(40) Duncan F———es, former Norwich defender.
(43) — City. Welsh club from Vetch Field.
(45) G—ld—t——— Ground (Brighton). Loop from the omissions.
(47) Leicester City play at Fi—b—r-- Street.
(48) Opposite of "heads".
(49) —Macari, Manchester United striker.
(50) — United, from Edgar Street Ground.
(51) England play here.
(52) Strangely, you can do this in the stand!

Down

(1) Footballer of the Year, 1965/66. (5 & 8)
(2) — Madrid. European Cup Finalists 1973/74.
(3) English Second Division Champions 1978/79. (7 & 6)
(4) Nottingham —, European Cup Winners 1979.
(5) Bring into working order by making arrangements.
(6) The time to decide after 90 minutes play.
(7) Tall structures for floodlighting.
(8) —p—tland; ground of Rochdale.
(10) ——rder Bremen; West German League club.
(11) Partick T———tle from Firhill Park.
(14) Feeling of uncertainty
(16) Wr—x—am play at the Race course Ground.
(18) For this a player can use his hands.
(20) Bjorn ——rdqvist (Sweden). World's most-capped player.
(24) — Gate, home of Bristol City.
(25) — Fife play at Bayview Park.
(27) They play at Oakwell.
(28) — Salvador; a World Cup participating country.
(30) — Park, home of Ayr United.
(31) ———bridge United were elected to the League in 1970.
(34) ——cre———on Park (Alloa). Angry from the missing letters.
(37) Take four letters from Crewe Alexandra to make a water-jug.
(38) — Villa, Birmingham club.
(39) ———n Cou—t, Bournemouth ground.
(41) Part played.
(42) ———tha— Crescent, York City ground.
(44) Helps or assists.
(46) He sits on the bench.
(50) R——ims. French 1955/56 European Cup Finalists.

Arab footballers not rich

Our Spanish correspondent ran into a team from Saudi Arabia in a Mediterranean hotel, he was surprised at the Arabs' reluctance to speak openly about football in their country — to the extreme that they prefer to remain anonymous.

Even so, some of the conversation threw some interesting light on the way soccer is run in the land where the likes of Rivelino pick up regal salaries in return for demonstrating some quality football.

"A lot of silly figures have been given for Rivelino's earnings at Hilal, and they create a false picture. I think he's earning about £10,000 a month, plus bonuses of about £100 for every match won.

"But don't get the impression that everyone earns that sort of money. The government only allows each club to have three professionals in the team, and in most clubs these tend to be players from Tunisia, Morocco or other Arab countries.

"It isn't easy to import non-Arab players because the clubs in Mecca, for example, can only have Moslem players on their books. At the moment there are only ten clubs in the first division, and they all receive grants from the government.

"At the beginning of each season each club receives £15,000 — and this figure is the same for all other sports as well. Then during the season the government runs a special points system. For example, if we invite a re-nowned foreign team to come and play us, that gives us a certain number of points. Then at the end of each season these 'merit points' are translated into cash.

"Our team hopes to raise a further £60,000 in this way. The government also pays 80 per cent of the salaries of the masseurs, secretaries and other staff — but again this is the same in all other sports clubs and isn't only true for football. When you add in our gate receipts, publicity contracts and so on, our total budget must come to about £750,000 or possibly £800,000.

"That may seem a lot of money to you, but I assure you soccer is pre-dominantly amateur, and there are only two professionals in our national team. We have no false pretences and no immediate ambitions for inter-national glory — we're just trying to learn the game and get our football properly organised right from the

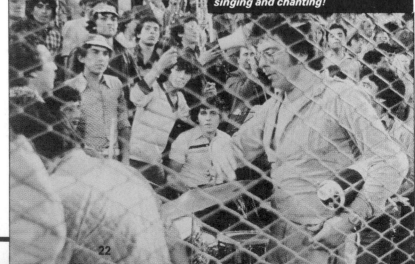
"Sheikh" Rivelino with his Arab bosses.

WORLD WIDE
compiled by CHRIS DAVIES

SPANISH club Córdoba gleefully pocketed more than £20,000 profit from a Cup tie against First Division Sevilla, but were lucky to hang on to the cash. One of the directors decided to take it home with him and go to the bank first thing in the morning . . . and during the night thieves broke into the club's offices, opened the safe and made off with the £1,250 that was left in it.

Chile fans certainly get behind their team. This picture shows a brass band, two drum sets and supporters with electric megaphones to lead the singing and chanting!

Football joke — Argentine style

Have you heard the latest soccer joke from Argentina?

A journalist, on his way to the River Plate v. Boca Juniors derby clash, saw a crowd gathered and stopped to see what was going on. He discovered a man terribly scratched, with clothes ripped to pieces. At his feet: a dead lion.

The reporter enquired what had happened. Apparently, the lion, who has escaped from a nearby circus, jumped out and attacked some children. The passer-by—on his way to the game—seeing the danger, went for the lion and after a tremendous scrap, managed to kill it.

The journalist took careful notes and the following day his story was published under the banner headline: "Cowardly River Plate Supporter Attacks and Kills Lion."

(The reporter was a Boca supporter!).

start.

"I'm sorry if we appear to be a little secretive, but we just want to get on with the job discreetly and not try to give the impression that we have petro-dollars to throw around left, right and centre. That's a totally false impression which we must try to correct."

Tarak of Tunisia attracted Arab interest after the 1978 World Cup.

Record sendings-off?

An almost certain world record has been set by the Pontes brothers in Brazil. Between them they have been sent-off the field on no less than 30 times between 1959 and 1978.

Daison Pontes has the worst record. A centre-back for many teams (he never stays for long!), he has been ordered off on 18 occasions, his offences ranging from fighting to ungentlemanly conduct and the use of stimulants.

His brother, Joao Pontes' (also his centre-back partner) record is a little better (!) "only" having been dismissed on 12 occasions mostly for insulting language to the referee!

Fortunately for the referees Daison retired from playing in 1976 following a suspension of 18 months.

However, Joao still continues to play.

Fear of flying

Terezo, a defender with the America club in Brazil, is terrified of flying. On their way to a game in the north, America manager sat down beside his player in the plane.

"Look son," he said, "the only real danger is taking off and landing."

Terezo went white and replied: "Thanks, boss, before I was just afraid of flying . . . now I have three fears!"

Flat-out and spot-on!

The River Plate/Velez Sarsfield tie had ended in a draw. Penalties would decide who would advance to the next round.

River's Argentina international goalkeeper Pato Fillol knew he held the trump card for his team's fate, so he stretched out on the ground for a minute before the penalty-decider to "concentrate and get in the right frame of mind."

It worked. Fillol saved two of Velez's spot-kicks (here he saves from Rotondi) and River won 4-3 on penalties.

Danish team-mates Henning Jensen (top) and Allan Simonsen.

Danes everywhere!

Denmark must surely be soccer's top exporters. Forty-two Danish players are playing abroad, literally all over the world as the chart below for 1979/80 reveals:

West Germany: 13

Carsten Neilsen	Mönchengladbach
Steen Tychosen	Mönchengladbach
Ole Rasmussen	Hertha Berlin
Henrik Agerbeck	Hertha Berlin
Soren Busk	Westfalia Herne
Jesper Petersen	FC Homburg
Jan Hojland	1860 Munich
Niels Poulsen	1860 Munich
Flemming Nielsen	Fortuna Cologne
Allan Hansen	Tennis Bor. Berlin
Jens Steffensen	Bayer Uerdingen
Niels Tune	FC St. Pauli
John Neilsen	Bremerhaven

Holland: 8

Henning Jensen	Ajax
Frank Arnesen	Ajax
Soren Lerby	Ajax
Jens Kolding	Roda
Jesper Rasmussen	Zwolle
John Frandsen	Zwolle
Kristen Nygaard	Alkmaar
Soren Lindsted	Twente

Belgium: 10

Birger Jensen	FC Bruges
Jan Sorensen	FC Bruges
Morten Olsen	Molenbeek
Preben Elkjær	Lokeren
Benny Nielsen	Anderlecht
Ulrich Tychosen	Royal Antwerp
Ib Jacquet	Royal Antwerp
Aage Hansen	Royal Antwerp
Soren Skov	Cercle Bruges
Erhard Auerbach	Cercle Bruges

Spain: 1

Allan Simonsen	Barcelona

Greece: 1

Ole Skouboe	Aris Saloniki

NASL: 4

Flemming Lund	Dallas Tornado
Henning Munk Jensen	San Jose Earthquakes
Ove Flindt	San Jose Earthquakes
Jorgen Kristensen	Chicago Sting

Austria: 3

Lars Francker	Rapid Wien
Keld Seneca	Sturm Graz
Niels Sorensen	Grazer AK

Switzerland: 1

Allan Michaelsen	Chiasso

Australia: 1

John Hansen	Hellas Melbourne.

Well done, pal! Glenn Hoddle of Spurs
congratulates Gerry Armstrong after the
Irish international had scored against
Brighton.

Congratulations

Aston Villa's Tony Morley is mobbed by
happy team-mates.

ABOVE
Derby County's Keith Osgood can't hide his delight following a goal for The Rams.
RIGHT
Wolves captain Emlyn Hughes has one of the most famous smiles in football. Here, he has good reason to laugh - John Richards has just scored.
BELOW
Terry McDermott looks as if he can hardly believe it, but a Liverpool goal is hardly a rare occurrence!

WAS PELÉ REALLY

Recent generations of soccer fans have been brought up on TV film of the great Pelé working unbelievable soccer wonders in that sensational Brazil team which won the 1970 World Cup in Mexico. We're all amazed by his skills, and practically all of us reckon that he's the best footballer of all time.

But is he? A recent international survey turned up a surprising number of votes for an Argentinian-born striker who dominated European football in the 1950s, wearing the all-white strip of Real Madrid—Alfredo di Stéfano.

Unlike Pelé, he didn't enjoy the benefits of world-wide TV coverage. Nor (thanks to untimely injuries) did he have the chance to hold the stage in a World Cup final.

But, if you get the chance, just have a look at film of the great Real Madrid side that won five consecutive European Cups—and judge for yourself who was the real Number One. Pelé? Or Alfredo Di Stéfano? And before you make up your mind, you might be interested to read what Bobby Charlton had to say about the two superstars in an interview originally published in South America . . .

'For a start, it's very difficult to judge two players who didn't play in the same position, nor at the same time. And we must remember that Pelé achieved his greatest popularity at a time when the whole world could watch him on television. Di Stéfano didn't have this advantage, and a large number of young people have never had the chance to see him in action.

Both had qualities, skill and personalities that made them into the idols of football fans. But, you know, the more I consider their respective merits over the whole of their careers, the more I'm inclined to go for Alfredo di Stéfano as my Number One.

Obviously both of them were phenomenal players, but in general I would say that de Stéfano was a creator *and* a finisher, whereas I feel that Pelé was basically more of a finisher. Obviously Pelé *did* do creative work, but I'm trying to pick out the essential difference between the two.

Di Stéfano was a creative genius. He was always giving good passes, make space, feeding his team-mates—and always with the ball perfectly controlled. On the other hand, Pelé almost invariably needed someone to supply him with good ball, and maybe if he hadn't had such excellent support from his team-mates, he wouldn't have stayed at the top for so long. Alfredo was a more complete player. He coud play in any position and he always knew exactly what he wanted and, more important, what his team-mates wanted. With Santos or Brazil, however, it was always up to the team to provide what Pelé wanted.

If it's difficult to differentiate between these two great players on the field, off the pitch they had one precious asset in common—a love of football that knew no bounds. Their greatness stems from the fact that neither played football for fame or fortune—they just wanted to play football. With success came the fame and the fortune, and they were welcome. But for them it was never the be-all and end-all. I remember that during the 1978 World Cup, Alfredo and I met up to hand out some prizes to the kids who'd won the Coca Cola skills competition. We were in the Ferro Carril Oeste stadium and Alfredo pointed to the railway tracks on the other side of the barriers. 'I used to run across that track and climb the wire barriers to get in here and kick a football around. In fact, I used to do anything to get a few minutes with a ball . . . '.

Alfredo had, I think, more of the qualities necessary to be a genuine leader of a football team. he was what we'd call an 'old pro' because he knew football inside-out. He knew all the tricks. And he never forgot that the important thing was the team—not individuals. I don't think that Pelé had quite the same qualities in this respect, even though he was captain of his club.

'I must admit that it was a mixture of pain and pleasure to play against either of these two. Pain, because you knew they were going to give you a hard time. And pleasure because it was always a joy to watch them in action. I actually played alongside Alfredo a couple of times, and he was still a sensational player after he'd retired and had developed quite a paunch! As opponents, we only crossed swords during the latter part of his career, and I'm happy to say that Real Madrid didn't always come out on top!

Playing against Pelé was a different matter, because it invariably meant that I was wearing the England shirt and playing against Brazil—which wasn't our favourite fixture by any means. I remember feeling doubly disappointed during the 1962 World Cup in Chile, because Pelé was ruled out of the game against us through injury. We lost 3-1 and I hadn't even had the chance to watch the great man at close quarters. I finally got my chance two years later in an international tournament in Brazil. They beat us 5-1, I'm sorry to say. I remember one moment during the second half when we were defending desperately. I saw Pelé running straight at me with the ball and I thought to myself 'now we'll see if he's really as hot as they make out'. A few seconds later I was sitting on the ground watching him let go a shot and shouting 'goal' at the same moment. I thought Pelé had gone mad, because I knew the whole England team stood between him and our goal. But when I looked round, there was the ball in the back of the net—he'd hammered it in from an incredible angle!

Di Stéfano also scored some spectacular goals in his time, but that was Pelé's speciality. He was a genius at beating opponents and putting the ball in the net. But I still maintain that Alfredo was the most complete player I've ever seen. Yes, *he* was the Number One. '

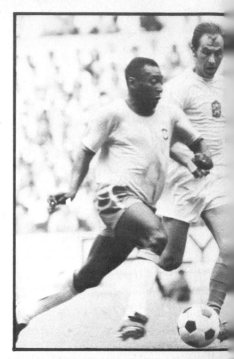

Former England star Bobby Charlton replies to the "Great Debate".

—WHAT THEY THOUGHT OF EACH OTHER—

Di Stefano on Pelé:

'Pelé had all the attributes of the unstoppable forward. He had thousands of variations in his repertoire, and all of them were exceptional. He shot with both feet; was an exceptional header of the ball; had a superb body-swerve; and wasn't afraid to go for goal from any angle. He was an electric player, always capable of opening up the path to goal in a split-second. It's easy to talk about Pelé, because you just run through the catalogue of footballing qualities and say that he had them all. He also had a strong will to win in addition to all his skills, and that was important. He was simply a phenomenal player—one of those players that I describe as having a 'fifth gear' that the ordinary player simply hasn't got.

I only played against him once, in an exhibition game in Madrid. Real beat Santos 5-3 that day. The most time I've ever spent with him was during the 1962 World Cup when both of us were out of action injured. We were both dying to play, but we just had to sit in the stand and bite our nails . . . '

THE NUMBER ONE?

LEFT . . . Pelé in action for Brazil during the 1970 World Cup Finals, when he was at his peak.
ABOVE . . . Alfredo di Stéfano tussles with Bobby Moore in the England v. Rest of the World game, 1963.

Pelé on di Stéfano:

I didn't see him play all that many times. Five or six maybe. The first time was in Europe in 1958, and the second a couple of years later when we were over there on tour. I was really impressed with him when Real Madrid beat us 5-3, even though we'd played 20 matches without defeat. He was a very complete player. Fast, intelligent and a good organiser of his team. The only fault I can find is that he didn't shoot very well with his left foot. But his greatest virtue was the way he set up non-stop attacks. He didn't wait for his team-mates to give him the ball—he went back and ran and sweated till he got it. Then he'd use it well, and set up a constant stream of chances for his team-mates. He wasn't bothered about scoring them himself. He just liked to see them go in. I always got on well with Alfredo, but people tell me he was a fiery character, and he used to give people a real roasting if they didn't come up to scratch. I learned a great deal from him—he's one of the greatest of the great players. ,

PHIL BOYER
-Southampton

'Manager Brian Clough tried to make me a right-winger'

Phil Boyer was wanted by both Derby and Forest as a youngster. He chose Derby, then managed by Brian Clough—and later thought he'd made a mistake.

Boyer, now with Southampton, says: "For some reason, Brian Clough saw me as a right-winger and I don't like playing there.

"He called me into the squad now and again as substitute but I never got on to the field.

"Eventually, York came in for me and Clough told me to either accept their offer or get used to playing in the reserves.

"I went—and began playing with a fella named Ted MacDougall. That's where my career really took off and since, of course, we've played together at Bournemouth, Norwich and Southampton.

"I probably learned most under John Bond at Bournemouth and Norwich. He's a great manager to play for and he taught me a lot about the game.

"Ted and I both benefitted from his advice and we rewarded him with plenty of goals.

"I'm still getting my share at Southampton. I have filled most positions up front.

"But despite what Brian Clough might think, I still don't see myself as a right-winger."

DAVID FAIRCLOUGH
Liverpool
'Came on as sub—and scored a U.E.F.A. Cup goal'

David Fairclough looks on as a happy Phil Neal displays his UEFA Cup winner's medal after Liverpool had beaten Bruges in 1976.

At the start of the 1975-6 season, David Fairclough thought he would do well to hold down a spot in Liverpool's reserve side.

But he made his debut three months into the season at Middlesbrough in a game Liverpool won 1-0.

"Two days later, I came on as substitute against San Sebastian in the UEFA Cup—and managed to score a goal".

Fairclough continued to keep coming off the sub's bench to score vital goals and end his first season with a League Championship medal, a UEFA Cup winner's medal—and another for helping the reserves to the Central League title.

"I've always got lots of goals, even when I was a kid. When I was nine, my dad and my cousin used to throw a ball at me to help strengthen my right foot because I was a natural left-footer.

"It did the trick. I'm now so strong on my right that I don't care which side the ball comes."

Liverpool first got interested in him after he'd scored all the goals in a local side's 8-0 win.

Ironically, he was brought up in the Liverpool suburb of Everton but he was always destined for Anfield.

"I kept hearing that clubs were interested in me but Liverpool were the only ones to come in."

BRIAN KIDD
– Everton

A 19-year-old Brian Kidd (left) after Manchester United's 1968 European Cup victory over Benfica.

'A European Cup Winner's Medal in My first season'

Brian Kidd describes his start to his first team career at Manchester United as "nothing short of a fairy tale."

At the start of the 1967-68 season, Kidd was an 18-year-old who used to look up to such stars as George Best, Bobby Charlton and Nobby Stiles.

He says: "I had no thoughts of a quick first team breakthrough, but I'd just got back from an England youth trip to Turkey when I was summoned to fly out on tour with the United squad the following day.

"They wanted another striker for the tour of America, Australia and New Zealand because David Herd had broken his leg.

"I did pretty well and when I came back, I was given my first representative game in the Charity Shield game against Spurs at Old Trafford.

"It was a pretty eventful debut. The game finished in a 3-3 draw and Pat Jennings scored for Spurs! He sent a high kick downfield which somehow bounced over Alex Stepney's head.

"Anyway, after that, I stayed in the team and the season ended, of course, with us winning the European Cup at Wembley.

"Just to complete the fairy tale, I scored one of the goals—and on my 19th birthday at that!"

GLENN HODDLE - Spurs

'I put a dream goal past Peter Shilton'

It must make Spurs shudder every time they recall that they once overlooked the skills of their England star Glenn Hoddle.

Says Hoddle: "They passed me over as a schoolboy and the only reason I got a second chance was that Martin Chivers came along to present the trophy at the Harrow schools cup final.

"He was so impressed by my performance that he recommended me to Tottenham and after a trial, they signed me on."

Hoddle will never forget that day—or his League debut against Stoke.

"I was a bit inhibited that day because I was pitted directly against Alan Hudson, who was one of my three heroes—Bobby Charlton and George Best were the others.

"Anyway, I did pretty well and everytime I did something right, Hudson would congratulate me.

"My debut was made a real dream when I put one past Peter Shilton from 25 yards. There aren't many players who can say they've beaten him from that range.

"The moment was made even sweeter by Hudson turning round to me and saying: 'I'll get a right rollicking now for not marking you more closely.'"

Middlesborough captain Tony McAndrew gets to the ball before Derby County's Ron Greenwood.

It's a Football Fact
TRANSFERS

Based on Baseball

The transfer system was first approved by the Football League in 1890. It was based on the system that already existed in America among professional baseball players in their National League which had been founded in 1871.

"Unsportsmanlike"

The F.A. tried to end transfer fees in 1894 and again in 1899, stating that "the practice of buying and selling players is unsportsmanlike and most objectionable." However, the system continued despite an effort to at least impose a transfer fee limit of only £10. In January 1908 the F.A. did in fact introduce a limit of £350, but this form of restriction on the clubs' transfer activities was so easily abused that it was withdrawn after less than four months.

Not Fit

In 1966 Huddersfield Town were instructed to refund £18,000 of the £30,000 paid to them by Blackburn Rovers for the transfer of Alan Gilliver in June that year, because it was found that he was suffering from disc trouble. This is nothing new. In 1894 Newton Heath (Manchester United) refused to pay Blackburn Rovers the transfer fee they had agreed for W.C. Campbell when they discovered that the player suffered from rheumatism. The amount involved was £25.

Q.P.R. Treble

Winger Mark Lazarus signed for Queen's Park Rangers on three separate occasions. Originally his transfer was secured from Leyton Orient during 1960-61, but he was sold to Wolverhampton Wanderers during the following season. However, he was transferred back to the Rangers at the end of that campaign and then went to Brentford in 1964, only to return to Q.P.R. in November 1965.

Favourite Graver

Centre-forward Andy Graver was a particular favourite with Lincoln City in the 1950s. He first joined them in September 1950 but transferred to Leicester City in December 1954. He didn't fit in there and Lincoln were glad to have him back at the end of the season. However, in November 1955, he was transferred to Stoke and subsequently played for Boston United before returning to Lincoln City for a third spell in October 1958.

£100 per Goal

Charlie Buchan was one of the cleverest and most artistic inside-forwards in the game's history. Indeed, there were those who considered that he was too clever and it was this that restricted his England appearances to six (plus one Victory game). A Londoner, he was transferred from Leyton to Sunderland in 1911 and helped the Roker Park club win the League Championship in 1912-13. When his playing career was drawing to a close, Arsenal obtained his transfer. The deal was an unusual one — Arsenal paid £2,000 and agreed to add a further £100 for each goal scored in his first season with them. He scored 22 and so the fee was more than doubled.

Signed During Game

Frank Laycock, one of Barrow's inside-forwards, was called off the field while playing in a Division III (North) game against Rotherham County in order for him to sign for Nelson. It was the last day for transfers that season — March 16th 1925 — and Nelson, in second position were pressing hard for promotion. Nelson finished runners-up to Darlington, but in those days only one club was promoted from each section of the Third Division.

Match Day Switch

One of the most remarkable transfers in the game's history occurred on February 7th 1925. Clapton Orient's centre-forward, Albert Pape, travelled to Manchester to play in a Second Division game against the United. However, two hours before the kick-off he was transferred to the Manchester club, and after the League had been contacted by telephone and sanctioned the move, he helped United defeat his old club, scoring once in a 4-2 victory.

8-Year Record

Since substantial amounts of money were first paid for players' transfers in the 1890s these fees have been continually on the increase and records are constantly being broken. The longest time a transfer fee has remained a record in Britain is just over eight years, and even that was due mainly to the intervention of World War Two. Eight years

Charlie Buchan (left) was the subject of a very unusual transfer. The transfer fee for Bryn Jones (above) established a record which stood for over eight years.

was the gap between the day in August 1938 when Arsenal shocked the football fraternity by paying £13,000 for Wolverhampton Wanderers' inside-forward, Bryn Jones, and September 1946 when Liverpool signed Newcastle United's red-haired centre-forward, Albert Stubbins, for £13,500.

Nottingham Forest defender Kenny Burns (red shirt) and Gerry Armstrong of Spurs in a mid-air collision.

NEIL ORR
Morton

"Same old fault. Doesn't get his body behind the ball."

"A new training idea. I've invented a ball that makes a whistling noise and you're going to save it by ear."

"Wait for it!"

PAUL HINSHELWOOD
Crystal Palace

39

Home is Easter Road for Peter Cormack

THE 14-year-old starlet had a spring and a bounce in his step that made Eddie Turnbull, who was then the Hibs coach, sit up and take notice.

He spent a lot of time with the youngster, working on his skills and developing his talents. The player went on to become a great favourite with the club, won representative honours for his country and collected two European badges in one of Britain's best-ever club sides.

His name? Peter Cormack. . .the same player who returned to Easter Road last season at the age of 33 on a free transfer from Bristol City.

"I've always loved Hibs, admits Peter. "I was sad when I left them for Nottingham Forest 11 years ago, but I wanted to sample English football. However, they were never far away from my thoughts.

"Even when I went to Liverpool I looked out for their results every Saturday. I had the opportunity to join my old mate John Toshack as a player/coach with Swansea and other clubs wanted me, too, but after I was freed by Bristol City there was only one team I wanted to go to— and that was Hibs.

"When they came in for me I was delighted to join them. I had a brief talk with Eddie Turnbull, who had first impressed me while he was the coach at Easter Road and I was a schoolboy going along for training.

"His knowledge of the game is immense. He knows football inside out."

Ironically, the pupil is now being tipped to take over from the master. Turnbull is likely to move out of the hot-seat at Easter Road and take up a backroom post in the near future and it looks as though Cormack is being groomed to take over.

Cormack signed a two year contract with the Hibs with the option of another two years as player/coach. Obviously he has designs on becoming a team-boss himself and it could be that he will get the opportunity to prove his ability as a manager with the club that has always been closest to his heart.

Bill Shankly, the man who paid out £110,000 to buy him from Nottingham Forest and take him to Liverpool where he won two UEFA Cup medals, says: "The boy has great determination.

"He always enjoyed his football. He had a natural enthusiasm for the game. He was the ideal player for Liverpool when I signed him. He wore the No. 5 shirt and played just in front of our back-four.

"And what a job he did for the club! I told Tommy Smith he should give half of his wage packet to Peter because he did half his work for him!"

Hibs will certainly need that sort of dedication and application if they are to make an impact in football again after the agonies of last season where their League form was nothing short of lamentable.

Cormack is currently enjoying a new lease of life, but he has a bone to pick with someone at Easter Road. . .coach Willie Ormond, who took a backroom job at Hibs after being sensationally sacked as Hearts manager last season.

"Willie never selected me for Scotland while he was manager," says Peter. "I often wondered why not. Now I have a great opportunity of asking him and finding out!"

The youthful Cormack has devoted himself to soccer as a player. Now that same sort of enthusiastic devotion looks likely to be taken to the managerial hot-seat. He could be a revelation in that role, too!

Andy Gray WRITES FOR YOU

"No time to think as Derby's Keith Osgood challenges."

"Why I have a short career"

THIS year saw my 25th birthday and I estimate I'll have another seven or maybe eight years left in football. As a striker, I'm fully aware that my career will be shorter than, say, a defender's. The fact is you don't find many 30-plus strikers in the First Division.

Players who have exceptionally long careers are usually goalkeepers or defenders, occasionally midfielders. Up front, you have to be razor-sharp, whereas further back you have more time to think and read the game.

In fact, by the time I reach my 30th birthday, soccer may have become so demanding that the retirement age is even lower. You'll find that over the years players have been hanging up their boots earlier and earlier.

At the moment, I can't see myself moving back to midfield or defence. I've been a striker all my career and, to be honest, I have no desire to play anywhere else. Andy Gray in the number four shirt just isn't on!

I must keep my sharpness. A striker lives on his ability to react in a split-second. In the penalty-box there is no time to think . . . you act instinctively. When this drops even marginally I know I'll have to think very seriously about my career.

Speed is the first thing to go when you reach the later stages, which is why forwards often decide to play deeper, where the physical side is less demanding.

There are exceptions to every rule and Ian Callaghan is one who springs to mind. Cally started as an out-and-out winger when Liverpool were making a name for themelves after winning promotion in the early 60's.

As football changed, so did Cally and as 1980 began he was still buzzing in Swansea City's midfield. I used to watch Ian when I was younger and marvel at his attitude and ability. If any SHOOT reader wanted to model himself on any professional, Ian Callaghan is the perfect example.

I doubt whether I'll be playing in the Football League when I'm in my late thirties. Right now I'm not TOO worried about my future. At 25, I must concentrate 100 per cent on football as I still have so much to (hopefully) achieve. My contract with Wolves ends when I'm 28 and then I'll sit down and give serious thought as to which direction I'll go.

If strikers don't have particularly long careers, they tend to be regarded as more glamorous than other players. Let's face it: those who score goals make the headlines. You can get more out of being a goalscorer, in this respect, than any other position.

Derek Dougan, the one-time Wolves favourite, played until he was in his mid-thirties and was rarely out of the headlines—for one reason or another. I remember The Doog as a real character; he once shaved his head and was always up to some caper. On the field he often appeared slow, but he combined well with John Richards and was deadly in the air.

To survive at the top a player must be

"Derek Dougan was rarely out of the headlines."

aware of his limitations and keep within them. It's no use trying to do things you can't. You must work hard and love the game, although only a very small percentage of professionals are in football for the money. And their careers are short, anyway.

You get nothing out of soccer unless you put a lot in. I'm full of admiration for the older players at Wolves, such as Emlyn Hughes, Willie Carr and Derek Parkin. They're the hardest trainers at the club and set a marvellous example to the younger players at Molineux.

I must confess I'm not the world's most enthusiastic of trainers. I'd rather play three games a week and not train! You'll never find me shirking, though. The more I put into training the better I'll play on Saturday.

When I was a teenager with Dundee United I remember Pat Gardner helping me a great deal. Pat was a striker, too, and spent many hours talking to me and giving me advice. I'll always be grateful to him. The manager, Jim McLean, once said something I'll never forget. It was during my first season when I was scoring freely and making a name for myself.

He called me in his office one day for a chat, and as I was leaving said: "Andy, never be content with what you achieve. Always strive for something better."

When I joined Aston Villa, the captain, Chris Nicholl, helped me in his own way. He knew how to wind me up and get the most out of me by geeing me up on the field. He was a first-class captain and I was fortunate to play under him upon starting my career with England.

The senior pro at Wolves is Emlyn Hughes and you won't come across a more enthusiastic player. Emlyn would be the first to admit he wasn't blessed with a great deal of skill, but his will-to-win and love of the game has made him one of English football's outstanding characters. We were delighted when he was awarded the O.B.E. What next? Sir Crazy Horse!

Some Scottish players return north of the border to finish their careers. I can't see myself doing this. I reckon I'll stay in England when my playing days are over, even though I couldn't say what I'll do. What I WON'T do is to be a coach or a manager. It just isn't me.

I was interested to hear some of the League's longest-servers, like Jack Charlton, Jimmy Dickinson and others say they felt they retired too early. It must be extremely difficult to make that final decision. I'd love to finish at the top as Denis Law did, but football can get to you and there must be a big temptation to carry on somewhere if a manager thinks you can do a job for him.

I imagine Billy Bremner enjoyed the final years with Hull, helping youngsters in the lower Divisions. I'll make that decision when the time comes, but in the meantime I hope you'll join me regularly in SHOOT.

Wolves midfielder Willie Carr on the ball.

Andy is watched closely by Arsenal's Willie Young.

43

Ted Drake, the former Chelsea manager and England centre-forward, nosed his saloon car to a gentle halt at the traffic lights.

Peter Sillett, Chelsea's sturdy England international right-back, was sitting comfortably in the passenger seat listening to the "boss" reflect on the pressures of running one of the biggest clubs in the country.

The car remained stationary at the traffic lights for FOUR minutes.

An exasperated policeman on foot patrol in the London suburb came over and said: "What's happening, driver? The lights have changed at least six times since you stopped."

Ted turned to Peter and said: "My God, Peter, I thought *you* were driving."

The tale is a favourite of Crystal

the lounge is the moment I revert to a routine even more enjoyable than football. That's when I assume the role of Family Man.

"Home life is important to me. All the worries disappear when I give my wife a kiss and start larking about with the girls.

"There are things more important in life than football. If you are not careful, the pressures of football can get to you. And that spells disaster.

"Home life should also be important to players, many of whom are single. I know of several footballers whose careers have been disrupted because they did not have a stable home life.

"Makes you wonder how much greater George Best might have been if

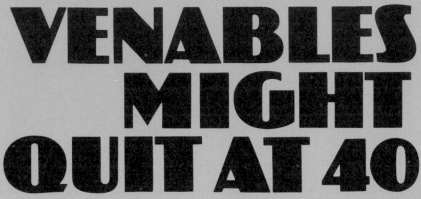

VENABLES MIGHT QUIT AT 40

Palace's manager and England Under-21 coach Terry Venables whenever he is quizzed about the enormous demands on a man chosen to run a football club.

"I told this old chestnut to the Palace side at a training session," grins Venables.

"Who are you trying to kid?", said Kenny Sansom, "the same thing happened when you drove me home the other day."

The Palace full-back was joking, yet no one is more aware than Terry Venables of the searching examination of character and endurance soccer management today imposes.

His escape is his family—and lovely home at Loughton, Essex.

Venables has never been one to mooch about the house in carpet slippers, ducking under the car bonnet on Sundays, whilst puffing gently on a pipe. But no one cherishes the privacy of a household more than Venables, one of the most outstanding young managers in the game, who suffered all the agonies of leading Palace into the First Division at the end of the 1978-79 session.

"I love football, but it might surprise people to know that once I step through the front door of my family home on a Saturday night, I try to forget all about the game," reveals Venables.

Wisecracking with his wife, Christine, and daughters Tracey and Nancy, is just as stimulating as leading a training session featuring some of the most promising young footballers in the country.

"I don't ever watch Match of the Day on television on Saturday nights. I video record it and watch it the next day!

"The moment I collapse on the sofa in

Terry's daughter Tracey wanted football boots on her birthday.

Fun at work (above) with Palace's England star Ken Sansom; Fun at home (left) with wife Christine; But not much fun for Ted Drake (right), at the traffic lights, when he managed Chelsea.

he had married early and gone back in the evenings to a home-produced stew.

"I was lucky. I married Christine at the age of 23. I first met my wife 22 years ago at the wedding of family friends in Dagenham, Essex.

"Allen Harris, my assistant at Palace, was best man. He is also godfather to Tracey, our youngest daughter.

"Christine has come to terms with being a 'football widow', but we make up for it in other ways. Football has often intervened at Christmas. Whilst other fathers are romping around the Christmas tree with their children, I have sometimes been tied-up on a football assignment, either as a manager or in my playing days at Chelsea, Tottenham and Queens Park Rangers.

"Fortunately, Christine understands because football has always been a part of our lives. I must confess that my wife and girls are not too enamoured with football. Tracey shows a bit of interest. She asked for boots and shin-pads on her tenth birthday.

"But Christine is not a regular at Palace's home games. She rarely watches and I don't thrust football down their throats when I'm home."

Venables believes that the neighbourhood a manager resides in is important to a happy home life. He has become one of the wealthiest young managers in the game, yet has chosen to remain on the East side of London all his life and has no plans to move.

"If you like a place there's no point in leaving it. I can never understand people who retire to the sea where they know no one.

"When I took over as Palace's manager from Malcolm Allison, I decided to give myself until 40 and then reassess my career. I might decide to leave the game or feel I can continue to make a contribution. We'll have to see. It worries me that managers can slip a little after reaching this milestone in life. I don't want that to happen to me."

Venables is fortunate to have more strings to his bow of talent than most other men in the game.

He runs pubs, businesses, and collaborated with Gordon Williams, author of Straw Dogs, the film, in writing the Hazell television series.

"All I want to do is to be able to choose what I want to do, when I want to do it, and have the freedom to carry it out.

"But at the moment I'm fully committed to the cause of winning things with Crystal Palace."

There are many experts predicting that Venables will one day manage England. Then the pressure will really be on . . .

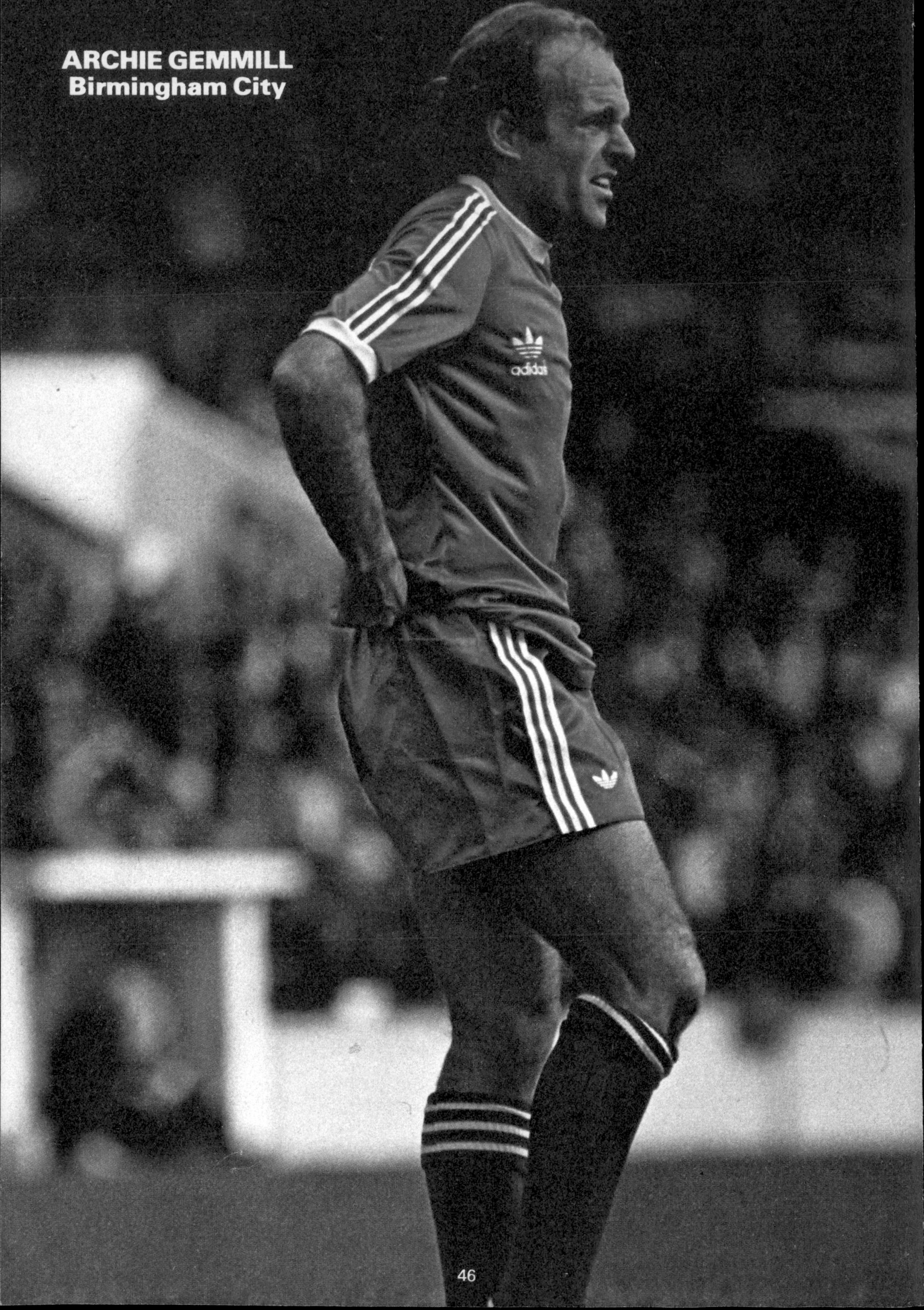

ARCHIE GEMMILL
Birmingham City

PAUL HART
Leeds Utd.

A look back at THE SEVENTIES

The last decade became the decade of one man and one team. Kevin Keegan was the player and Liverpool the club.

The brilliant Dutchman Johan Cruyff and Franz "Kaiser" Beckenbauer were still mighty forces in World football during this era, but their international careers had started before 1970.

Kevin Keegan was kicking a football for Scunthorpe when they had become established stars, but from the moment Bill Shankly spotted Keegan's potential and took him to Anfield, Keegan and the mighty "Reds" were destined to make a hefty impression on British soccer history.

They *were* the Seventies so far as the average football fan was concerned.

They dominated television, newspapers and advertising hoardings with their superb displays, culminating in Liverpool's glorious European Cup Final win over Borussia Moenchengladbach in Rome in 1976-77. Terry McDermott, Tommy Smith and a Phil Neal penalty sank the Germans.

A season later Liverpool did it again, beating F.C. Bruges 1-0 at Wembley through a goal by Kenny Dalglish, their brilliant Scottish international striker.

Liverpool and Keegan imposed a stranglehold on the First Division Championship. They were Champions, in 1973, 1976, 1977 and 1979; runners-up in 1974, 1975 and 1978; and won the F.A. Cup in 1974 and were runners-up in 1971 and 1977.

It was hardly surprising then that Kevin Keegan was to become the hottest property in European football after Liverpool's European Cup victory in 1977.

The Great Man decided to leave the club which had given him his chance. He felt there was nothing more he could achieve in the North-East. They had won everything and he was as much a part of British soccer folklore as Stan Matthews, Tom Finney, Bobby Charlton, Jimmy Greaves, George Best and Denis Law.

He was transferred to Hamburg S.V. for £500,000, the highest fee involving a British club. Almost in the same breath, Liverpool wasted not a second in finding

The night Kevin Keegan became world-class . . . his 1977 European Cup Final performance for Liverpool against Borussia Mönchengladbach will never be forgotten.

Kev's replacement. He came in the stocky frame of Kenny Dalglish, a £440,000 buy from Celtic but a snip by today's inflationary standards.

England's opening games of the decade saw other great stars still in command. The two Bobbies, Charlton and Moore, were each destined to pass Billy Wright's record of 105 England caps, while Gordon Banks would clearly have emulated their feat had he not lost the sight of an eye in a tragic car accident.

Fortunately for England, we have always been rich in goalkeepers and Ray Clemence and Peter Shilton emerged to share his yellow jersey with distinction.

England's record at international level was undistinguished for much of the Seventies. They failed to qualify for the 1974 World Cup 12 years after winning the trophy, and Alf Ramsey, the hero of English football in 1966, lost his job as England's manager.

Joe Mercer took the reins briefly until a successor could be found. The chosen one was Don Revie, who had guided Leeds United to heights previously unscaled at Elland Road.

The choice was misguided. He adopted stifling negative tactics which did much to destroy the credibility of football as an entertainment for supporters.

They played across the pitch instead of making thrusting, penetrating runs and despite the stirring contributions of Kevin Keegan and the emergence of Trevor Francis, Dave Watson, Mick Mills, Phil Thompson, Peter Barnes and a host of other promising recruits, Revie's reign did nothing to enhance the Seventies at international level.

There were few tears when he resigned to seek a fortune in the United Arab Emirates where his vast knowledge has had some impact.

The opening of the decade was fine for English clubs. For the first three years we took both the European Cup Winners' and UEFA or Fairs Cups.

Worked Miracles

Club-wise at home it was a period of change. Leeds United, managed by Revie and captained by the fiery Scottish international Billy Bremner were in decline after several masterful seasons in which Norman Hunter, Allan Clarke, Eddie Gray, Paul Madeley, Johnny Giles and Jack Charlton had become household names.

Switch on the telly and there were Leeds United in action. Now, came Liverpool's turn. Bill Shankly guided Liverpool to the top with a mixture of soccer expertise allied to an enormous capacity to get the best from players such as Emlyn Hughes, Peter Thompson, John Toshack, Steve Heighway and 'Mighty Mouse'' Keegan.

His retirement in 1974 was mourned at Anfield but not for long, for Bob Paisley, Shankly's shadow for many years, slipped easily into the chair.

Meanwhile, a man named Brian Clough was working miracles at Derby County with players such as Roy McFarland, Colin Todd, Archie Gemmill and Kevin Hector.

It was brash management. Unpredictable, eminently suitable to Fleet Street columns and popular with his players.

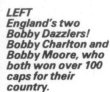

LEFT
England's two Bobby Dazzlers! Bobby Charlton and Bobby Moore, who both won over 100 caps for their country.

RIGHT
Northern Ireland's most-capped player, Pat Jennings, saves against Scotland in 1972.

BELOW
Thanks, Shanks! Another Championship for Liverpool and the one and only Bill Shankly.

Derby County 58 points, Leeds, Liverpool, Manchester City 57 — the League Championship went to the Baseball Ground in 1971-72. And again under Dave Mackay in 1974-75.

Meanwhile, transfer fees were soaring. On New Year's Day 1970, the record British transfer was still the £165,000

Leeds had handed Leicester for Allan Clarke six months earlier.

On January 1st, 1980, Wolves had broken the transfer record by splashing out £1½ million on Andy Gray, Aston Villa's Scottish international striker.

League clubs soared up and down the divisions as if they were suspended by elastic. Huddersfield, for instance, were of First Division status in 1970. Five years later they had plummeted to the Fourth.

Nottingham Forest languished in the Second Division for much of the Seventies but up popped Brian Clough again to guide them to promotion in 1976-77.

The following season they swept to the First Division title, accumulating 64 points to Liverpool's 57 in second place. They lost only three games that season.

"Grass Roots"

Hooliganism increased despite vast efforts by League clubs to curb the anti-social behaviour of mindless morons. The dart, better employed in public bars of pubs, were thrown at goalkeepers, and other objects were hurled from the terraces.

'Cage them in,'' said the experts. And that's what happened. New regulations governing safety measures at grounds were imposed. They were costly but for once clubs were forced to spend money on equipment rather than flesh.

It was inevitable that clubs should be asked to tighten-up after the Ibrox disaster in 1971 when 66 died at a Rangers-Celtic derby.

Prominent in England sides at the start of the decade were Emlyn Hughes, Martin Peters, Alan Ball, Allan Clarke and Roy McFarland. All were still playing in 1979-80.

Northern Ireland's remarkable goal-keeper Pat Jennings was still performing wonders for his country at the end of the Seventies after making his international debut in 1964. Ian Callaghan, once of Liverpool, was still going strong

at Swansea, revitalised by the management of John Toshack. Apart from Alan Dicks (Bristol City) and Bobby Robson (Ipswich) not one First Division club had the same manager in 1980 they had on New Year's day 1970.

But if managers were dispensed with, directors tended to stick.

One player made more debuts and departures than a conjurer's rabbit. George Best. He walked out of Manchester United for the last time in 1974, flirted briefly with Fulham before choosing to pursue a career in the United States.

In November 1979 he signed for Hibernian at the age of 33. By February 1980 he had walked out on them, confessing to a drink problem. He made contact with Alcoholics Anonymous and received the sympathy of all those who had warmed to his brilliance in the 1960's. He remained a drawing card but those who had seen the brilliant Irishman at his best could never accept George Best mark II.

The decade drew to a close on a high note. England qualified for the European Championships with the best record of any country, under the management of Ron Greenwood.

Where once Don Revie had highlighted the paucity of talent, Greenwood examined the "grass roots" of the game as well as taking charge of the national side.

"It's not that bad", seemed to be his message. Glenn Hoddle, Bryan Robson, Graham Rix, Ken Sansom and Tony Woodcock, who went from Forest to Cologne, emerged and the pundits were predicting a brighter Eighties than Seventies.

No one was arguing, especially after Kevin Keegan, England's favourite son and twice European Footballer of the Year in 1979 and 1980, announced his transfer from Hamburg to Southampton.

Keegan, the player who threaded gold through the often bleak Seventies, had sent British football spinning into the Eighties on the crest of a wave.

DOUBLE TROUBLE FOR CLARKE

The popular trend over the past few years has been for British players to go abroad to find fame and fortune. Ray Clarke is an exception to that; he had three season in Holland and four months in Belgium before deciding to end his European adventure and sign for Brighton.

In fairness, Clarke was not making much progress in England earlier in his career. He'd been rejected by Spurs, and went to Swindon and Mansfield before his goals in the lower Divisions made people notice him.

There was talk of a transfer to a big English club, but the Mansfield manager at the time, Billy Bingham, left the club and Clarke's possible departure was on ice.

Then, in the summer of 1976, Sparta Rotterdam contacted Mansfield about their English striker.

"It was a complete surprise," he says. "I wasn't thinking in terms of the Continent. I flew over to Holland the next day, though, to see what Sparta had to offer.

"The idea of leaving England and all our friends didn't really appeal to me. Sparta's offer was too good to turn down. They paid me six times what Mansfield were; I signed the same day.

"On the way home I began to wonder if I'd made the right decision.

"There were problems. There always will be, with the language, finding accommodation, making new friends. You have to change your lifestyle completely.

"Luckily, I was scoring a few goals, so this helped. I made up my mind to learn Dutch, even though I knew I wouldn't be in Holland too long. Everyone there speaks English, anyway. Once people realised I was making an effort they accepted me readily."

Clarke's goals made him one of the most feared men in the Dutch League and when Ajax sold Ruud Geels in 1978, the man they chose to replace their star goalscorer was Clarke. In April, he joined the Amsterdammers for £225,000, a huge fee by Dutch standards.

The goals kept coming and Clarke was Ajax's top scorer in 1978/79, helping them to win the League and Cup double.

It wasn't all good times for the Clarkes, however. Ray, his wife Cindy, and their two children found the strain of him playing for such a big club immense.

'Owned me'

Ajax would keep a tight control over his off-field movements, even checking what time he went to bed.

"They were a very 'political' club with some strong personalities. Some of the things that went on were unbelievable.

"Okay, they paid me well, but they thought they owned me. I remember coming home one evening and Leigh, my four-year old son, said to me: 'Daddy, how long do you have to play football for?'

"I told him I was doing a job to get the best for the family. Leigh then said: 'I'll take a bomb and blow up Ajax.'

"When a four-year-old talks like that you start to worry. We wanted to come home to England."

Instead of returning, Clarke moved on to Belgium in the summer of 1979 when FC Bruges paid £200,000 for him.

"I decided to have one more year abroad to ensure by the time we went back we'd be financially secure. After three years in Holland, I thought another 12 months in Belgium would be easy. It was like starting all over again. When Brighton made their offer I couldn't sign quickly enough."

Bruges got their money back in October, 1979, and Clarke played his part in helping Brighton retain their First Division status, even though at one time they looked certs for the drop.

Fighting off relegation was a far cry from winning the Double with three-times European Cup winners Ajax, but Ray Clarke loved every minute of it.

IT'S A DIRTY GAME

ABOVE . . . Bad weather doesn't stop Crystal Palace goalkeeper John Burridge from enjoying training.
RIGHT . . . Who cares about the mud when you've scored? Tony Woodcock doesn't after netting for England in Northern Ireland.

LEFT . . . Stoke strong man Denis Smith has broken dozens of bones, so a bit of rain is hardly likely to bother him.
BELOW . . . Sheffield Wednesday's Terry Curran shows he's no stick-in-the-mud by scoring against Bury.

LAUGH LINE

"If they lose this one they're doomed for relegation."

"Don't worry about cooking a meal, dear—I've had a knuckle sandwich."

"I read in the papers that our defence was torn to pieces by their forwards last Saturday, Bert."

OF DEFENCE

"And I say that last goal was caused by the bad understanding between you couple of layabouts."

"I've just worked out why they paid a million pounds for that striker, Charlie."

BUY your pesetas, polish up on geography, dust down the rattles and claxons, don scarves and coloured woolly hats—the 1982 World Cup is gathering momentum.

A record number of 24 countries will contest this prestigious soccer jamboree in Spain.

It poses important questions. Can Argentina maintain their hold on the trophy after winning the 11th World Cup Final in their home country in 1978, or were the performances of Mario Kempes and Osvaldo Ardiles a flash in the pan?

Can Holland re-establish themselves as a force after reaching successive World Cup Finals in 1974 and 1978 or has "Total Football" disintegrated?

Will West Germany impose their customary authority on the competition? Can England blossom again after failing to quality in 1974 and 1978?

The unique pull of the World Cup is that all these questions and many more will remain massive imponderables until the last shot is fired in anger at the end of the World Cup Final.

The competition's history is littered with upsets; the emergence of underdogs, the collapse of favourites; tears and elation . . .

It is compelling entertainment and the 12th World Cup in the land of cheap package holidays promises to be no exception. But then it has been that way since the last World War.

For proof, simply study our potted history

THE GREATEST SOCCER SHOW ON EARTH

1950 in Brazil

A disappointing entry after a 12-year break in the World Cup enforced by the Second World War. The competition was played on a League format and late withdrawals did not help to re-establish the world's greatest soccer tournament.

England's powerful squad included the legendary Stan Matthews, Tom Finney and Wilf Mannion yet they were to figure in one of the biggest upsets in soccer history after beating Chile 2-0.

The scoreline which shook the world read: United States 1, England 0.

No one gave the Americans a chance. Some of their squad had gone to a party the night before the match — but the incredible happened at Belo Horizonte. Bahr crossed and Gaetjens headed the winner in the 37th minute.

Brazil, the favourites, met Uruguay, their biggest rivals, in a game that would decide the Championship. Brazil led after two minutes through winger Friaca, but Varela, Uruguay's outstanding defender, was beginning to impose his authority. Schiaffino equalised and Ghiggia scored the winner 11 minutes from time. Brazil had already written a song to celebrate their anticipated victory, and even worse, some fanatics, unable to cope with the shock, jumped out of windows.

The best team in the competition had lost!

Goal-hero Gaetjens.

winners Uruguay

1954 in Switzerland

Hungary had emerged as a new soccer power. They were dubbed the "Magnificent Magyars" after tearing England apart at Wembley in November 1953 and 7-1 in Budapest the following May.

The world eagerly awaited the World Cup debuts of Ferenc Puskas, a captain with a matchless left foot; Josef Boszik, a parliamentarian and educated winghalf; Nandor Hidegkuti, a deep-lying centre-forward and Sandor Kocsis.

The competition was played in four qualifying groups with a knock-out from the Quarter-Finals.

The scoreline read incredibly: Hungary 8, West Germany 3. Kocsis scored four goals.

Scotland were massacred by Uruguay on their World Cup debut but England

reached the Quarter-Finals before going out 4-2 to Uruguay. Hungary and Brazil were to figure in the most disgraceful game ever seen -- the notorious "Battle of Berne".

Hungary led West Germany 2-0 after

eight minutes in the Final but Morlock and Rahn equalised. Hungary missed chances and Rahn scored the winner for West Germany 15 minutes from the end. A late goal by Puskas was disallowed and Turek saved brilliantly from Czibor.

Germany celebrate a Final goal.

winners West Germany

1958 in Sweden

The balance of world soccer swept away from Europe — to Brazil. An unknown 17-year-old named Pele made his debut for them.

England's best performance was to hold Brazil to a goalless draw and Northern Ireland, who had disposed of Italy in qualifying earned a creditable draw with West Germany thanks largely to superb goalkeeping by Harry Gregg. Wales drew with Sweden but Scotland were put out by France.

A goal by Pele disposed of Wales in the Quarter-Finals and Northern Ireland slumped 4-0 to the French.

It looked as if Sweden would produce another upset in the Final when they led Brazil 1-0 through Liedholm after four minutes. Now, Brazil began to buzz. "Little Bird" Garrincha swept through Sweden's defence twice to lay on goals for Vava, Pele scored twice and left winger Zagalo completed the scoring.

Pelé makes his mark with a goal.

The best team had won this time and a man who was to carve himself a unique place in world soccer had started his international career in storybook style.

Pele went on to become a legend, lifting Brazil to glorious success and carving himself a place in history.

It says everything about him that Pele went on to help his country win the Cup twice more.

winners Brazil

1962 in Chile

The Brazilian and Czech captains before the kick-off.

Brazil, the holders, brought the nucleus of the great side they had sent to Sweden four years before. They opened with a 2-0 win over Mexico with goals from Zagalo and Pele, but in the next match against Czechoslovakia they lost Pele with a badly-damaged muscle, an injury which kept him out of the rest of the tournament.

Brazil reached the Quarter-Finals before coming up against Brazil in Vina del Mar. Garrincha outjumped Maurice Norman to head Brazil's first goal. England equalised through Gerry Hitchens but Peter Springett, England's goalkeeper, could not hold a swerving Garrincha free kick and Vava scored.

Garrincha himself scored the third.

Brazil beat Chile 4-2 in the Semi-Finals and Czechoslovakia swept into the Final with a 3-1 victory over Yugoslavia.

Brazil were given an early shock when Masopust snapped up Scherer's measured pass to put the Czechs ahead but a mistake by Schroiff, the Czechs goalkeeper, let in Amarildo for the equaliser. Then Zito scored and just before the end Djalma Santos hoisted a lob into the Czech goalmouth, Schroiff "lost" the ball in the sun and Vava scored Brazil's third goal.

Brazil, even without Pele, had proved too good for the best of Europe.

winners Brazil

1966 in England

The competition marked the decline of Brazil and the emergence of a brilliant Portuguese striker, Eusebio, who scored nine goals in the competition.

North Korea did the "impossible" by defeating Italy and then gave Portugal a fright. England's manager Alf Ramsey described Argentina as "animals" after Bobby Moore's team had beaten the South Americans 1-0 at Wembley. Rattin had been sent-off, eight minutes elapsing before he left the pitch.

England met Portugal in the Semi-Final and Bobby Charlton scored two goals to put the home country into the Final for the first time. England's other man of the match was Charlton's Manchester United team-mate Nobby Stiles, who stuck to Eusebio like a limpet.

The Final between England and the old enemy West Germany was pulsating. Wembley was packed and 400,000,000 watched on television.

Haller shot the Germans ahead but Geoff Hurst equalised with a header. Martin Peters seemed to have clinched victory with a volley 12 minutes from time but in the last minute Jack Charlton fouled Held and Weber equalised from the free kick. Extra-time.

"You've won it once. Now go out and win it again!" Ramsey told his men.

Alan Ball ran himself into the ground and Geoff Hurst went on to write himself into history by scoring a hat-trick.

Geoff Hurst's controversial goal.

winners England

1970 in Mexico

Now, could England prove themselves worthy Champions 'away' from home, or would Brazil re-establish themselves with Pele, Tostao and Jairzinho inspiring a new generation of Brazilians.

West Germany were fancied with Beckenbauer and Overath in the team and Italy relied heavily on the Cagliari striker Luigi Riva.

Many thought England's early game against Brazil to be a rehearsal for the Final. It was goalless at half-time thanks to one of the greatest saves in World Cup history from Gordon Banks. Jairzinho's cross was met squarely by Pele's head but Banks twisted backwards to scoop the ball over the bar. Pele was flabbergasted — and applauded. But Jairzinho scored the winner.

England accompanied Brazil into the Quarter-Finals by beating the Czechs through Allan Clarke's penalty. Banks was not fit for the match against West Germany and his deputy, Peter Bonetti, was wrongly criticised for at least one of the Germans' three goals, Muller volleyed the winner after both Martin Peters and Bobby Charlton had been substituted.

Brazil went on to beat Italy 4-1 in the Final and thus keep the Jules Rimet trophy for winning it for a record third time.

Football of a superb pedigree!

Gordon Banks' miracle save from Pelé.

winners Brazil

1974 in West Germany

Franz Beckenbauer

So, a new World Cup and Finals organised, and eventually won, with typical Germanic efficiency by the host country.

England had not made the finals, but Scotland were there with the blessing of every football fan in Britain. They felt they had a real chance with an opener against Zaire. But this was where they faltered. It was to be a group where the three top teams drew against each other. So goals against Zaire were vital. Scotland managed only two, Brazil three and the Yugoslavs nine. It proved no consolation to Scotland that they were the moral victors against Brazil and Yugoslavia. They were eliminated on goal difference, the only unbeaten side in the tournament.

Holland and West Germany met in the Final. Ninety seconds had elapsed before the Dutch were awarded a penalty when Cruyff was brought down by Hoeness as he darted through the German defence. English referee Jack Taylor had no hesitation in pointing to the spot — and Neeskens scored.

Midway through the first half West Germany equalised from a penalty through Breitner and six minutes later they scored what proved to be the winner. Bonhof surged forward and crossed to Muller who, at the second attempt, hooked his shot beyond Jongbloed.

Holland dominated the second-half but the glory belonged to Franz Beckenbauer and his team.

winners West Germany

1978 in Argentina

Argentina became the third host country to win the World Cup in the last four tournaments.

They were fancied to do well from the start but produced a brand of exciting football through the superb skills of Kempes, Ardiles, Bertoni, Luque, Passarella and Fillol which their countrymen had never seen.

By the time they reached the Final where they met Holland in Buenos Aires on June 25, 1978, their fame had spread to every soccer loving country across the world.

They scored through Kempes in the first-half but Nanninga equalised for Holland. Then the brilliant Rensenbrink hit a post but the match went to extra-time.

Now, the Argentinians turned on full power before 70,000 fans. Kempes scored again and Bertoni put the game beyond the Dutchmen's reach.

The competition was remembered for some brilliant goals. The shooting power of Haan, Dirceu and Cubillas was unforgettable.

British interests had faded early after the removal of Scotland. But the Scots did partially redeem themselves by beating Holland 3-2 in their last match.

Happy Argentina after scoring against Holland.

winners Argentina

ON 26th May, 1967, Billy McNeill held the European Cup high above his head in Lisbon's national stadium. Celtic had beaten Inter-Milan to become the first British team to win the trophy.

Now 14 years later Billy McNeill is manager of the club he skippered to victory that historic, glorious night.

Manager at the time was, of course, the great Jock Stein. He believed in attack and positive football even from his defenders Billy McNeill and Tommy Gemmell, the full-back who scored Celtic's equaliser with a 20-yard thunderbolt shot after Mazzola had given Inter the lead with a penalty.

Jim Craig and John Clark, McNeill's assistant-manager today, completed a formidable rearguard in front of the still agile 36-year-old 'keeper Ronnie Simpson.

In midfield there was the magic of Bertie Auld and Bobby Murdoch. Up front winger Jimmy Johnstone was unbeatable and sprayed passes to Willie Wallace, Bobby Lennox and Steve

LEFT . . . Former Celtic player and manager Jimmy McGrory.
RIGHT . . . The Big Man—Jock Stein.

CELTIC
HEADING FOR
NEW GLORY

Celtic's most successful captain of all-time and now their manager: Billy McNeill.

Chalmers, the scorer of Celtic's winner five minutes from time.

After the match the stadium was a sea of green, white and tartan as Celtic fans celebrated victory. That night Lisbon belonged to them.

There are few fans as passionate as those who follow Celtic, probably one reason why the club has had so much success over the years.

But winning honours wasn't even a dream when the club was formed in 1888 to provide soup kitchens for Glasgow's poor.

Celtic Football and Athletic Club began life in style, beating Rangers (who'd been in existence for 15 years), 5-2.

A year later Celtic attracted more attention by reaching the Scottish Cup Final, losing 2-1 to Third Lanark.

They finally won the trophy for the first time in 1892, beating Queens Park — still the only non-professional club in Britain — 5-1.

That was to be the first of many triumphs for the club that has always been compared with their Glasgow neighbours Rangers.

The Old Firm have never hidden their religious differences. While Rangers would never knowingly employ a Catholic, Celtic have no such restrictions.

Indeed, some of their most famous players have been Protestants . . . so too was the man who led them on to great heights. . .Jock Stein.

CONTINUED OVER

On his appointment as manager in 1965, he told reporters: "You're respected for what you do — not your religion. Why, most of Celtic's managers have been non-Catholics!"

The comment brought laughter because Stein was only the club's fourth boss and every one had been a former player.

The first was Willie Maley, a stern, brusque figure. He played in Celtic's first match and went on to serve the club for over 50 years.

Maley was succeeded by Jimmy McStay. Then came Jimmy McGrory, the greatest goalscorer in Scotland's history.

It was in 1936, helped by a record 50 goals from McGrory, that Celtic won their first Championship for ten years, finishing five points clear of Rangers.

The following season they won the Cup, and in 1938 their Jubilee Year, the title again and the Exhibition Trophy, which involved Everton, Sunderland, Chelsea, Brentford, Hearts, Rangers and Aberdeen.

The suspension of football during the Second World War halted the club's progress, and the seven years afterwards was the worst period in their history. The only success was a Cup win over Motherwell in 1951.

But victory in the Coronation Cup of 1953 which included Arsenal, Manchester United, Spurs, Newcastle, Rangers, Hibernian and Aberdeen — proved to be the turning point.

Celtic were then captained by Jock Stein. After seven seasons with Albion Rovers he left in 1949 to play non-league football in Wales.

Two years later he agreed to go back to Parkhead as skipper of the reserves.

In 1953-54, Stein, Bobby Evans and Bertie Peacock inspired the club's first League and Cup double for 40 years, but the next Championship didn't come for another 12 years, when Stein was manager.

Hearts and Rangers dominated Scottish football during the late 1950's and early 1960's and Celtic's only worthwhile achievement during that time was a 7-1 League Cup Final win in 1957-58 against Rangers.

Wee Bobby Collins was the inspiration of that side. Jock Stein's career had already been ended by injury. In 1956 he became club coach then left to serve his managerial apprenticeship with Dunfermline and Hibs. He returned to Celtic as manager on 9th March, 1965.

During Stein's reign Celtic became one of the best, most feared teams in the world. Under The Big Man they won ten League titles — including a world record nine in succession — eight Scottish Cup and six League Cup triumphs.

But his greatest moment was undoubtedly beating Inter-Milan in Lisbon.

"The European Cup is the big one," he said. "This is only for the best — for

60

Champions."

Celtic had competed in Europe before that, of course. In Stein's first season as manager they reached the Semi-Final of the Cup Winners' Cup before losing by a single goal to Liverpool.

In 1969 Celtic became the first British team to reach the European Cup Final for the second time. After beating Leeds in a superb Semi-Final they lost 2-1 to Feyenoord in the Final in Milan.

The following season Feyenoord's Dutch rivals Ajax dumped Celtic out of Europe. It was then Jock Stein knew he would have to rebuild.

Into the reckoning came youngsters Lou Macari, Kenny Dalglish, David Hay, Vic Davidson, Ally Hunter, George

Celtic won the Top Ten in 1976-77 with a 1-0 win over Hibernian. . . the goal scored by Joe Craig.

Rangers dominated the scene in 1977-78 after completing the Grand Slam. But the season had started badly for Parkhead fans when their hero Kenny Dalglish was transferred to Liverpool for £440,000.

Then in May, 1978, a few days after ex-skipper John Greig had replaced Jock Wallace as Manager at Ibrox, Billy McNeill announced he was leaving Aberdeen to take over from Jock Stein at Celtic.

In his first season in charge Celts clinched the Premier Division Championship again, with a sensational end of season victory over Rangers. That made success even sweeter.

McNeill had arrived — so had new faces like Murdo McLeod, from Dumbarton, Davie Provan from Kilmarnock and Dom Sullivan from Aberdeen.

Brilliantly skippered by Danny McGrain in defence, with the drive of Roy Aitken in midfield and George McCluskey up front, Celtic are surely destined for another age of silver trophies, despite losing the 1980 title to Aberdeen.

Celtic stars of yesterday and today . . .
Kenny Dalglish (left), Don Sullivan
(right) and Danny McGrain (below).

Connelly and Danny McGrain.

As these players matured Celtic continued to find success on the domestic front, until their sensational record-breaking run was brought to a halt by Rangers in 1974-75.

But even then you couldn't keep the Parkhead men out of the limelight. To soften the blow of losing the title Celtic captured the Scottish and League Cups.

Stars at Hampden when they beat Airdrie in the Scottish Cup Final were Kenny Dalglish and Billy McNeill. It was his last game after 18 glorious years at the top.

The following season saw a dramatic change in Scottish football with the introduction of the Premier Division. Rangers were the first winners.

Who will be the

Peering into the misty depths of a crystal ball for a look into the future is as much a favourite pastime of soccer fans as it is of wizened old gipsy women encamped in small tents at fairgrounds.

It was fairly predictable that Leeds United would carry on the good work they had accomplished in the late Sixties. Many of the players who guided them to the League Championship in 1968-69 were still heavily involved and likely to be so for the next five or six years.

But few would have predicted Arsenal's progress in clinching the title in 1970-71 — Leeds United came second — and winning the F.A. Cup to emulate Tottenham's "double" winning performance of a decade earlier.

Liverpool were clearly going to be a side to be reckoned with under Bill Shankly's mercurial direction but who would have given Derby County a price in pulling off the First Division title in 1971-72, and again three seasons later?

Similarly, Nottingham Forest's chances of becoming anything more than a steady Second Division team were redundant, but such is the great uncertainty of football that Brian Clough led them not only to the 1977-78 League Championship but to the most coveted club prize of all, the European Cup in 1979 by courtesy of the only

goal of the game from Trevor Francis.

The start of the new decade has encouraged the experts and the not-so-experts to play the guessing game again.

Who will be the teams of the Eighties?

Ipswich Town, under Bobby Robson's direction, are the popular choice to do well on the strength of their performances in 1979-80.

The East Anglian club have shed the unfashionable image which seems to haunt clubs who play their football outside the big cities.

Certainly, the form of Alan Brazil, the leadership of Mick Mills, the defensive skills of Russell Osman and Terry Butcher and the exciting front running of Paul Mariner render them a force to be reckoned with.

But if it was necessary to plumb for an "outsider" who had done nothing in the Seventies to indicate success in the Eighties, then Coventry City would be a fair bet for honours with their precious cargo of young stars.

Gordon Milne, their mentor and former Liverpool half-back, regularly fielded six players under the age of 21 in the 1979-80 season.

Tom English, who once equalled Jimmy Greaves's record of scoring five goals in a County Boys game, is a thoroughbred striker capable of giving most First Division defences a run around.

He signed pro forms in the summer

team of the '80's ?

Blair could become etched on the minds of the average Eighties fan as Dalglish, Hughes, Heighway and Clemence had done in the previous decade.

Coventry's young lions have sprung to the fore at the same time, just as Chelsea's "chicks" and Busby's "Babes" had done before them.

What hope these final placings in 1982-83: 1 Coventry, 2 Ipswich 3 Middlesbrough.

A revival in the North-East is long overdue. Newcastle United would be most people's choice to recapture their glory years of 30 years ago but another candidate for attention is Middlesbrough the most improved First Division team in the North.

The Ayresome Park club were once dubbed the most boring team in the land. They talked of Mannion and Hardwick as if they were still wearing the red jersey, but that was understandable because of the lack of success since their retirements.

'Boro revival

John Neal's arrival as manager from Wrexham in succession to Jack Charlton prompted a revival — and suddenly the team took on a new shape.

Mark Proctor, David Hodgson and captain Tony McAndrew seem destined to lead a revival.

Crystal Palace were unfairly labelled the "Team of the Eighties" as the first half of the 1979-80 season drew to a close.

It seemed a shrewd observation with Terry Venables young team doing well in the first season back in the First Division. But a string of injuries to Gerry Francis, Mike Flanagan and Ken Sansom, their new England left-back, threw a cloak of doubt over their progress.

Venables clearly needs to spend money to add a dash of talent to an already talented stable of youngsters, but their turn will come again.

No club grew more tired than Aston Villa of the title "Yesterday's Team". The once great club has achieved little since the Second World War, yet Ron Saunders is piloting a revival of fortunes with one of the best crop of youngsters in the country.

Allan Evans, Terry Donovan, Gary Shaw and Des Bremner are names which seem capable of carrying Villa to the success their fans have yearned for.

Similarly, Birmingham City seem capable of springing surprises under Jim Smith's guidance. He is one of the shrewdest tacticians in the game and is adopting the same formula at St. Andrews he used to such stunning effect at Blackburn.

A long shot? Portsmouth, First Division champions in 1949-50, but chopping blocks for most clubs since. Now, Frank Burrows is beginning to work a mini-revival which, given time, could blossom into a major resurgence of power for the club.

Meanwhile, Liverpool, Arsenal, and Forest will no doubt carry on the good work they started in the Seventies.

ABOVE
Both Liverpool and Coventry should be successful this decade.
LEFT
Dave Swindlehurst scores for Crystal Palace against Manchester City.
BELOW
Aston Villa's goalscoring defender Allan Evans heads home a Cup goal against Cambridge.

of 1979 and looks certain to win England honours if he maintains his progress.

Garry Thompson is another from the top drawer. Born in Birmingham he ousted the high-scoring Mick Ferguson from the team but broke a leg. However, he was back to his best in 1979-80 and has the right pedigree to go right to the top. Nicky Phillips, Ray Gooding, Paul Dyson, Gary Gillespie, widely tipped to captain Scotland one day, and Andy

Few footballers have made a greater impact on the First Division at the start of their football careers than Manchester City's centre-half Tommy Caton.

City's chief coach Malcolm Allison was in raptures about his new defender within hours of Caton's debut at the start of the 1979-80 season.

"He'll be an England player before long," said Allison emphatically.

But for once Big Mal was beaten to the gun. Tony Book, City's general manager, was preaching the gospel according to the Maghull, Liverpool born

decision, for few rising young stars in England have attracted the attentions of foreign clubs more than he.

Allison is not short of words on the subject of the centre-half. "I've never seen a boy with his physique. In training, he performs every bit as well as experienced pros. He was competing with everybody else from the first day he was here."

He is also modest. After playing against Liverpool, he said: "Kenny Dalglish is the best player I've marked. I say marked. I hardly got near him."

LIVERPOOL EVERTON MAN UTD

WHY TOMMY REJECTED THEM FOR CITY

youngster 18 months before Allison.

"I don't usually go overboard about a youngster but Tommy is a special case. He has a lot of ability and with natural development, should be knocking on the first team door at 18."

Prophetic words from the Maine Road chief. Indeed, Tommy barged right through the first team dressing-room door to line-up in a shirt worn previously by Dave Watson within a month of signing professional forms at the start of the 1979-80 season.

Manchester's leading sports writers were scrambling for comparisons. Was he as good as Duncan Edwards, Manchester United's England star who died tragically in the Munich air crash?

But the majority preferred to accept that Manchester City had produced a youngster capable of bridging the yawning gap between schools football and the Football League in months rather than years.

An indication of the size of Caton's impact on the First Division is that no one mourned the departure of Dave Watson from Manchester City.

It said something of his potential when City were thrusting a contract at him after just 10 first team games which would have bound him to the club for life.

And it says much of his maturing awareness of the pitfalls in soccer that he politely declined the invitation, stating: "Although at the moment I feel happy at the prospect of staying with City much longer, there must have been a time when Peter Barnes and Gary Owen felt the same way."

So, Caton has kept his options open. He is unlikely to be disappointed by his

Long after his debut Caton claimed he was still playing for his first team place, taking nothing for granted.

He has inherited that unassuming attitude from his father, Tommy senior, a local government officer.

"I know Tommy has got it, but you have to keep on at him. The thinking is that he won't have any regrets if he doesn't achieve all his ambitions."

He was given little option but to remain level-headed at Maine Road. Despite his first team place, until he reached his 17th birthday, he performed the same menial duties as every other apprentice on the staff.

He was born on Merseyside and chased by a multitude of big clubs before signing for Manchester City. Liverpool, Everton and Manchester United all came for him, but although Caton had stood for years on the terraces at Anfield with a Liverpool scarf protecting him from the North-West's icy winter blasts, he had no intention of joining them.

"The way they groom players at Anfield, I reckoned it was going to take me a long time to make it and it could have been the same with the other clubs," he said.

His family emigrated to Australia at one time. He was chosen for Australia's Under-13 national side — as an inside left.

He has never made the mistake of ignoring his studies at the expense of football. He holds seven GCE "O" levels and is taking "A" level maths with an eye to securing a safe job should his football career be cut short.

The World Cup Finals in Spain in 1982 could provide a marvellous platform for him to parade his exceptional talents.

Most soccer fans can remember who scored the winning goal in the F.A. Cup Final, but the player who laid on the telling pass is invariably forgotten.

When Ipswich Town beat Arsenal in the 1978 Wembley Final, it was Roger Osborne who became the hero of East Anglia. . . yet it was a beautifully controlled run and centre from David Geddis that made Osborne's goal possible.

Geddis, in fact, didn't think he would line-up against Arsenal. Town manager Bobby Robson was facing a direct choice between Geddis and Trevor Whymark.

Just before the Final, Ipswich played Aston Villa — the Final Test some called it — but Villa were in rampant form and ran out 6-1 winners.

Although Geddis scored Ipswich's consolation goal, he was certain he'd lost out in his battle to play in the Final. Now, as he looks back to that game in the claret and blue of Villa, he can see the irony of it all.

"I was so thrilled to be called up. It was like a fairy tale. Yet I travelled half way round the world just to be a substitute. We arrived in New Zealand, but by then I'd picked up a back injury and had to return home.

"The summer rest cured that, then I was hurt in pre-season. That kept me out for five months — a thigh injury it was. Just as I was getting fit, I was involved in a car crash, which meant almost two months on the sidelines.

"I just didn't have a chance. I was always trying to get fit, but there was setback after setback. The side was doing quite well without me and Ipswich qualified for Europe again.

"When 1979/80 began, I had a chat with Mr Robson, because I was fully fit and eager to play. He told me my prospects weren't bright and a transfer was the best solution.

"I didn't enjoy playing in the reserves. I was, however, aware that clubs were looking at me, so I did my best. Villa came in for me and I was happy to sign.

"They had a young side, with three or four new faces. Taking over from Andy Gray didn't worry me. Fans have to accept players in their own right. What did bother me was taking so long to get off the mark. When my goal went in against Spurs after three months it was a huge relief.

"Brian Little and I built up an understanding fairly quickly. We complement each other. He has the close control and flair, I provide the hustle and bustle.

"Although things went a bit sour at the end, I enjoyed my spell with Ipswich. They're a well-run club who have made the most of their resources. Considering their location, it's little short of a miracle the way they've kept pace with the 'big boys'.

"Villa, on the other hand, are a big club in every sense of the word. The stadium, set-up, fans . . . everything is geared towards success. I just hope I can be part of it."

Villa almost robbed David of Wembley glory

"It would have been a twist of fate if my present club had robbed me of a winners' medal, " he says. "Luckily for me, Bobby Robson had a special role for me against Arsenal, almost as a right-winger.

"With Clive Woods on the left, this meant we could stretch the Arsenal back-four. It was my first-ever visit to Wembley. The manager's tactics paid off and it was a marvellous debut for me."

Following the Final, Geddis, then 19, was selected for the England "B" tour of the Far East.

Geddis in action for Villa . . . and against Arsenal in the F.A. Cup Final at Wembley.

Rangers' Kenny Watson in Old Firm action watched by team-mate Colin Jackson and Celtic's Roy Aitken.

LUTHER BLISSETT
Watford

PUZZLE

PICK YOUR OWN SIDE

Select just one letter from each horizontal row so as to spell out the names of a dozen English or Scottish League sides. As a guide, ALDERSHOT is indicated for you.

A	L	N	L	M	B	R	B	B	D	D	C
E	L	O	R	I	L	A	E	O	U	L	L
V	A	D	T	E	A	I	N	N	M	Y	W
H	C	N	C	B	S	E	C	C	E	D	C
E	F	T	R	K	E	A	R	A	E	A	K
F	P	B	S	S	I	S	R	S	B	P	R
O	T	U	T	H	T	O	A	T	O	E	H
A	O	R	R	E	L	E	O	O	N	L	Q
R	D	N	L	R	T	N	D	E	L	K	M

SOCCER CIRCLES

Find the correct starting points in each of the circles and, moving onto alternate spaces in a clockwise direction, spell out the names of six soccer teams, two in each of the three rings.

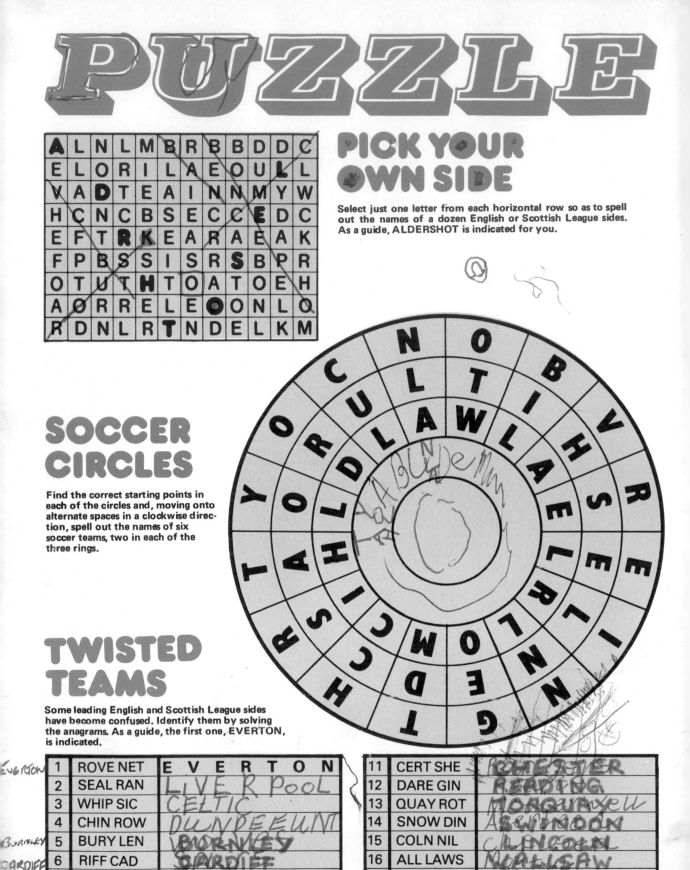

TWISTED TEAMS

Some leading English and Scottish League sides have become confused. Identify them by solving the anagrams. As a guide, the first one, EVERTON, is indicated.

#	Clue	Answer
1	ROVE NET	E V E R T O N
2	SEAL RAN	LIVERPOOL
3	WHIP SIC	CELTIC
4	CHIN ROW	DUNDEE UNT
5	BURY LEN	BURNLEY
6	RIFF CAD	CARDIFF
7	LES ACHE	CHELSEA
8	RON STEP	PRESTON
9	FAT WORD	WATFORD
10	ASS WANE	SWANSEA

#	Clue	Answer
11	CERT SHE	CHESTER
12	DARE GIN	READING
13	QUAY ROT	MORGANXELL
14	SNOW DIN	SWINDON
15	COLN NIL	LINCOLN
16	ALL LAWS	WALSALL
17	HEN CRIB	St Mirrin
18	WEB RICK	BERWICK
19	ERR SANG	RANGERS
20	KIP CART	watford

68

~TIME

ANSWERS ON PAGE 80.

BACKS TO THE FRONT...

... not a new role for soccer defenders, but a novel type of crossword in which, instead of clues across and down, you have them backwards and upwards. As a guide, the first backwards and upwards clues are solved for you. All the clues have a soccer flavour.

BACKWARDS:

1 Every manager hopes for one
2 Remains of hope after Cup defeat
4 Injury means this for many
6 Hoped-for game in Cup draw
7 Madrid's actual team
8 Giants do this to small fry
9 Teams do this with each other
14 They play at Filbert Street.

UPWARDS:

2 All hope to be this kind of forward
3 A score in "that other game"
5 Tigers is their club nickname
10 The Merry Millers of the League
11 A cup fixture not necessarily a draw
12 Bad showing means this in the cup
13 This on pitch can ruin game
14 They are kings of the Kop.

... but it is not Cup or League problems that have them confused. Just a game of anagrams. Unscramble the letters of each name to identify 12 English League managers. As a guide, the first, TERRY VENABLES, is indicated for you. Now get cracking on the remainder.

MANAGERIAL MIX~UP

1	ALBERT SEVENRY	TERRY VENABLES
2	LAURY ELLMAN	Liverpool
3	DONALD ISCOIN	CELTIC
4	BOY TOKON	TONY BOOK
5	PETER ECHOYEGG	WOLVES
6	BRIAN CHUGAL	Spurs

7	JACK HOTNOSH	Brighton
8	ALBIE KIEMY	Arsenal
9	ROD ARIADIG	Bristol City
10	DAN VEXTOES	Everton
11	SAMMY MADJOIN	Rangers
12	MORT THEYMYCOD	Hearts

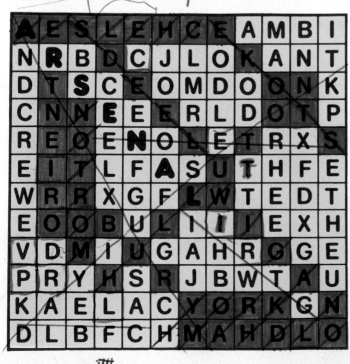

TEAM WORK

The name of no fewer than 20 English or Scottish football teams are spelt out in this frame, either horizontally, vertically or diagonally, forwards or backwards. As a guide, ARSENAL is indicated for you. See how many others you can spot.

~~HHH~~ I
~~HHH~~

RIDDLE~ME~ RHYME

Kick this hard, you can't go wrong;
Then add an ad and make a song.

69

STEVE DALEY
Man. City

JOE JORDAN
Man. Utd.

71

ABOVE . . . Austria's Karl
Stotz chooses a
matching hat and scarf to
keep warm.
BELOW . . . César Menotti
of Argentina was given
this cap by a fan and has
worn it regularly ever
since.

IF THE HAT FITS . . .

Many players are
identified by a
particular gimmick. A
certain wave, how they
celebrate a goal, or
simply the way they
look. Some of the
international
managers are, it would
appear, opting for
headwear as their
trademark.

RIGHT . . . This cap may not
be typically Brazilian, but
their former manager
Cláudio Coutinho often
seemed to prefer a European
style of play for his teams.
BELOW . . . Enzo Bearzot of
Italy prefers the traditional
soccer bobble hat to keep
out the cold.

RIGHT . . . France
manager Michel
Hidalgo dressed
for the occasion
during the 1978
World Cup in
Argentina.

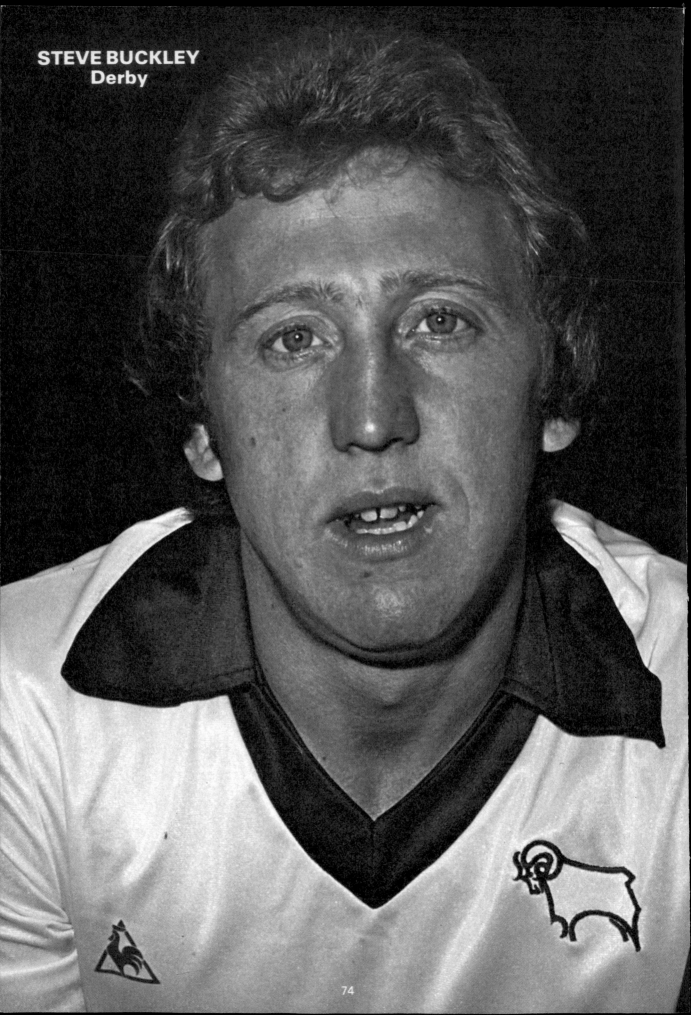

STEVE BUCKLEY
Derby

74

PHIL PARKES
West Ham

THE growl was unmistakable and the accent was porridge-thick. Bill Shankly, who now ranks alongside Robert The Bruce and William Wallace among the list of legendary Scots, was talking about his favourite subject . . . football.

OBVIOUSLY the topic got round to his first love Liverpool and their conquering of Europe in successive season—'77-'78 and '78-'79—by beating West Germany's Borussia Munchengladbach and Bruges in consecutive Finals.

However, Shankly decided to pay homage to Celtic instead for the major part they played in the European Cup by making the breakthrough as long ago as '67 when they travelled to Lisbon and turned the game upside-down by defeating the club outside Celtic and Rangers. It's a case of being safe rather than spectacular."

Those are hardly words of an adventurous manager, but his outlook must be appreciated and there can be little doubt that the Premier Division is putting extreme strain on bosses and players.

"A club such as Celtic must look to Europe," says Parkhead manager Billy McNeill. "We have a huge following throughout the world and it is imperative that we are seen to be doing well on this front. Of course that puts added pressure on us, but everyone at Celtic Park must learn to live with that pressure."

Celtic, who came so close to winning the European Cup again in '70 before going down to a last-minute goal in extra-time to Feyenoord, look to be Scotland's best bet in the near future to break through again.

When Jock Stein took over Celtic in 1965 the team was struggling. He guided them to a Scottish Cup triumph—with the remarkable Billy McNeill heading the winner in a 3-2 win over Dunfermline at Hampden— and two years later he had moulded them into the masters of Europe.

McNeill took over the team from Stein in

So, Celtic obviously have the potential to do something on the European circuit in the coming seasons. Rangers, too, have had encouraging results on this front although failing to make the most of their opportunities.

Last year they knocked out Fortuna Dusseldorf from the Cup-Winners' Cup and then drew 1-1 with Valencia in Spain. Alarmingly, though, after having done the hard work well, they sat back at Ibrox and lost 3-1! That is a mistake that cannot be repeated.

John Greig, like his good rival McNeill, has had his career sprinkled with champagne. He is ambitious, go-ahead and knowledgeable and he is determined to emulate Celtic by lifting the Champions Trophy.

Realistically, though, the economics of the Scottish game means that the best players will almost certainly be sold if a big-money cheque is waved under the nose of some pressurised manager. It is difficult, to say the least, to build a solid foundation from which to launch an assault on Europe in this climate.

"Like Celtic, we also have a world-wide

CAN SCOTTISH CLUBS

defensive experts of Inter-Milan by 2-1 on a brilliant, sunny evening on May 25.

"Jock Stein and Celtic showed the other British sides that it could be done," points out the former Anfield supremo. "We should never forget what they did. No one had done it before and someone had to get over that hurdle to show the others what it was all about.

"Celtic led the way for others to follow. They were the trail-blazers, if you like. a year later Manchester United beat Benfica at Wembley to pick up the trophy and the ball was well and truly rolling after that. Celtic, though, were the team the others followed in crashing that barrier."

The words of Shankly are welcome to long-suffering Scottish fans. In the last decade there hasn't been an awful lot for them to get excited about in European warfare. Rangers won the Cup-Winners' Cup in 1972, but other results have hardly been awe-inspiring.

Rangers did well two years ago to reach the Quarter Finals of Europe's premier tournament after beating Juventus and PSV Eindhoven, but they were narrowly beaten by Cologne, who, in turn, went out to eventual winners Nottingham Forest in the Semi-Finals.

But apart from that bright and too-brief sortie, the other performances have been about as enjoyable as a swim with a few piranha fish for company.

Can things get better? Will Scotland be able to go proudly into Europe in the coming seasons? Will a Scottish club conquer Europe again?

On the club scene one manager, who obviously wants to remain obvious, says: "Europe? I haven't got time to give it a thought. There is so much pressure at home with the Premier Division that I have got to get things right here.

"It would be nice to do something in Europe, of course, but domestic football is our bread and butter, don't forget. Relegation could mean disaster for every

similar circumstances a few seasons ago. They had just completed a disastrous term in which they had won nothing and they had even failed to qualify for Europe for the first time in 14 years.

He started again and obviously he has learned a thing or two from Stein, now, of course, the international supremo. Celtic are on the right lines with some exciting players such as the serpentine-weaving Davie Provan, an entrancing winger, Roy Aitken, a power-house in midfield and defence, Murdo MacLeod, known to his team-mates as 'Rhino' because of the way he charges around all day, breaking up attacks and setting his team mates on the way with glorious passes. Danny McGrain, too, has a lot to offer and goalkeeper Peter Latchford is one of the best in Britain.

Fortuna Dusseldorf v. Aberdeen in the 1978/79 UEFA Cup.

John Greig after Rangers' Cup Winners' Cup triumph.

following and they expect you to do well in the big European tournaments," says John Greig. "There can be no falling off of standards. You must keep on trying to produce the goods.

"Is the Premier Division too competitive? Certainly it's a difficult League and there are no so-called 'easy' fixtures, that's for sure. But we have always taken every fixture as it has come along and tried to win it.

"It doesn't matter who we play we always give them the utmost respect. We treat everyone like they could be Bayern Munich, Real Madrid or Ajax. That's the attitude I had as a player and I'm not going to change it now.

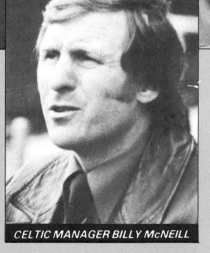

Celtic's Lisbon Lions with the 1967 European Cup.

RULE EUROPE?

"Yes, Europe is vital for Rangers and other Scottish clubs. A victory in these tournaments can really 'lift' the game back home."

The Old Firm, then, know they must contribute something before Scottish clubs lose their credibility in this soccer hot-bed. What about the other teams?

Aberdeen have often threatened to do things in recent years, but have always fallen when it looks as though they have got into their stride. Three years ago they had a good goalless draw in Belgium against the highly-rated RWD Molenbeek, but lost in the second leg at Pittodrie. They followed this up by giving Fortuna Dusseldorf a three-goal start the year after that before

winning 2-0 in Scotland and coming so close for forcing the game into extra-time.

Fortuna went on to reach the Final of the tournament that year and were very unfortunate to lose to Barcelona in extra-time. Last season they drew 1-1 with Eintracht Frankfurt at Pittodrie and then dominated the return game in West Germany much to the surprise of the home fans. However, their courage wasn't rewarded and a single goal from Bernd Holzenbein took Eintracht through.

With a bit of luck Aberdeen could do something providing manager Alex Ferguson can keep his best players. In the past The Dons have been forced to part company with players such as Joe Harper—who later returned—Martin Buchan, Zoltan Varga, Steve Murray, Tommy Craig and Jimmy Smith just when things have been looking good.

"I want players who want to play for this club," says manager Ferguson forcibly. "I want them to be proud to be an Aberdeen player and wear that red shirt."

If Fergie can get the attitude right there can be little doubt that Aberdeen will become a force to be reckoned with. Every Scottish fan certainly hopes so because the St. Andrew's flag obviously needs good standard-bearers.

Scotland's other main hope for success in this field must be Dundee United, but their efforts in Europe over the past decade have been nothing short of lamentable. Possibly last season's League Cup triumph will give their players a bit more belief in their ability. It could be that once they have crashed the psychological barrier they can go on from there.

One thing is abundantly plain: Scotland cannot afford to lose their way in European football and become a third class soccer nation. They need to be seen to be successful and the sooner they get things sorted out, the better it will be for their game.

And what about the Scottish inter-

national team? They were a disaster area in the World Cup Finals in Argentina in '78 and the year after that was another dreadful period for the players and Jock Stein.

In fact, taking every nation's results that year into account, Scotland finished a miserable twenty-first in the European table.

That's a statistic that is not designed to keep the fans following their national side. They played eight games that year and managed to win only two—against Northern Ireland and Norway—and they lost four with two being drawn. A harsh, shameful fact.

Why can a nation provide players such as Kenny Dalglish, Graeme Souness, Alan Hansen, John Robertson, Davie Provan, Roy Aitken, Derek Johnstone, Danny McGrain, Martin Buchan, Gordon McQueen, Joe Jordan, Andy Gray and countless other soccer gems fail to make the big-time and make their presence felt? Why, indeed, have they never qualified for the European Championship Finals?

Those are other questions that will have to be answered. AND SOON!

Strain is the name of this particular game, but success in Europe is never achieved without a lot of pain. It's worth it when it all comes right at the end of the day.

Just as Jock Stein and those eleven Celtic players of 1967. Scottish football yearns for a repeat . . .

CELTIC MANAGER BILLY McNEILL

MICK CHANNON
Southampton

78

LAURIE CUNNINGHAM
Real Madrid

Butcher's no hatchet-man

With a name like Butcher, you could be forgiven for thinking the Ipswich Town defender is always out for opposing forwards' blood. Terry is anything but a hatchet-man. In fact, when he first came into the Portman Road side there were fears he wasn't hard enough!

"Opponents took advantage of my inexperience," he says. "They'd use every trick in the book to put me off my game. I'd take far more 'stick' than I ever dished out.

"I soon learnt how to look after myself and keep my concentration."

At 6'4" and close on 14 stone, Butcher certainly had the necessary build for a defender. He's also two-footed . . . thanks to an accident as a youngster.

"I hurt my right foot, so I used to kick with my left. Now, if anything, my left foot is the stronger."

This versatility has helped Butcher, who can play anywhere across the back-four, although he sees himself as a sweeper, eventually.

Terry came into the Ipswich side during 1978, against Everton at Goodison Park and since then has been a regular, either at centre-half, sweeper or left-back.

"Allan Hunter and Kevin Beattie were having a bad time with injuries," he says. "I got my chance. The big test came when all of us were fully fit, but touch wood I've managed to stay in the side.

"I was born in Singapore, but grew up in Lowestoft, and always dreamed of being a professional. Even now I sometimes have to pinch myself to see if it's all true. Ipswich were the team I supported as a lad and when they offered me terms I jumped at the opportunity to join them.

"I'd virtually decided to further my education at college. Then Ipswich stepped in."

Butcher quickly made an impression in the first team, and after a dozen or so games, manager Bobby Robson was heard to say: "Terry looks as if he's been around for years. He's playing against players with far more experience, but you'd never notice the difference."

Terry went on the England tour during the summer of 1979 and thought he would play for the Under-21's.

He wasn't selected for the first match, in Bulgaria, and assumed his chance would come in Sweden.

"I was in for a shock — a very pleasant one, however. Ron Greenwood selected me for the "B" side to play Austria. Unfortunately, there was an electric storm early in the second-half and the game was abandoned. Even so, it was great simply to be chosen."

Many people feel Terry could be the player to eventually succeed Dave Watson into the full England team.

"I've got a long way to go before I can start thinking of that," says Butcher.

"I've enjoyed playing for the Under-21's and 'B' sides, mixing with older players, listening and learning. I'd be lying if I said it wasn't my ambition to progress to the senior side. All I can do is to play my best for Ipswich and hope for the best.

"Mick Mills has helped me a lot. He's been around for ages and is a model professional. I watch him in training and his attitude is first-class. He hardly ever has a bad game.

"Allan Hunter, too, has given me a lot of good advice. As a centre-half, he knows my problems better than anyone."

Terry Butcher may have a long way to go, but he could arrive sooner than he thinks!

On top . . . that's Terry Butcher.

Answers to puzzle-time

TEAM WORK:
Alloa: Arsenal: Ayr: Bury: Chelsea: Clyde: Crewe: Derby: Exeter: Hull: Leeds: Luton: Morton: Oldham: Orient: Oxford: Raith: Stoke: Wigan: York.

SOCCER CIRCLES:
Outer ring: BRIGHTON, COVENTRY.
Inter ring: CARLISLE, SOUTHEND.
Inner ring: MILLWALL, ROCHDALE.

TWISTED TEAMS:

1. Everton	14. Swindon
2. Arsenal	8. Preston	15. Lincoln
3. Ipswich	9. Watford	16. Walsall
4. Norwich	10. Swansea	17. Brechin
5. Burnley	11. Chester	18. Berwich
6. Cardiff	12. Reading	19. Rangers
7. Chelsea	13. Torquay	20. Partick

PICK YOUR OWN TEAM:
Aldershot: Blackburn: Blackpool: Brentford: Clydebank: Doncaster: Dumbarton: Leicester: Liverpool: Mansfield: Newcastle: Rotherham.

MANAGERIAL MIX-UP:
1. Terry Venables (Crystal Palace)
2. Alan Mullery (Brighton)
3. Colin Addison (Derby)
4. Tony Book (Manchester City)
5. George Petchey (Millwall)
6. Brian Clough (Nottingham Forest)
7. John Toshack (Swansea)
8. Mike Bailey (Charlton)
9. Dario Gradi (Wimbledon)
10. Dave Sexton (Manchester United)
11. Jimmy Adamson (Leeds United)
12. Tommy Docherty (Queen's Park Rangers).

BACKS TO THE FRONT:
Backwards: 1. Loyal team: 2. Ash: 4. Out: 6. Home: 7. Real: 8. Eat: 9. Vie: 14: Leicester.
Upwards: 2. Ace: 3. Try: 5. Hull: 10. Rotherham: 11. Tie: 12. Exit: 13. Ice: 14. Liverpool.

RIDDLE-ME-RHYME:
BALL-AD.

JOHN ROBERTSON- *the Forest master*

John Robertson picked up the ball just outside the opponents' penalty-area. A flick of the hips and he was round his marker. A glance up told him the 'keeper was just a fraction off his line. With the most delicate of chips, Robbo lofted the ball over the 'keeper's arms into the top corner of the net. A wonderful goal, the sort the Continentals usually score.

"Surprised? Me? No. That's what I expect of The Master," said Nottingham Forest assistant-manager Peter Taylor afterwards.

The Master — that's what they call John Robertson at the City Ground. Brian Clough goes one better and says he's the best at his job in the world.

It was Robertson's inch-perfect cross that enabled Trevor Francis to win the European Cup for Forest against Malmö in 1979.

Most teams pay Robbo the compliment of putting TWO markers

on him — a midfield player and a full-back. If he beats one, he then has to get past another . . . which he often does.

Robertson is one of the few players who can cause a buzz of anticipation around the terraces. With him, the unexpected has become the expected!

All a far cry from the player's early days with Forest when he was a midfield-man under Dave Mackay. When Mackay left for Derby, Allan Brown took over and Robbo found himself in the reserves more often than not.

"There were times when I was convinced I'd be leaving Forest," Robertson remembers." I was just drifting along going nowhere. Then Brian Clough and Peter Taylor arrived and everything changed.

"Whatever I've acheived in the game must be down to them. Without their help and encouragement I'd be a nobody. They altered my attitude, my whole approach to the game, and made me into a winger.

"For one reason or another, we were short of someone to play wide in one particular match and the manager asked me to do this job. Wingers had gone out of fashion after England's 1966 World Cup win, but were slowly coming back into the game.

"I didn't really think I had the speed to be a winger. The management worked on all aspects of my game, both physically and mentally. I remember Peter Taylor once gave me a right dressing-down in front of the others. Looking back, he was right . . . I'd become complacent."

Robertson was still relatively unknown when Forest won promotion to the First Division — but not for long.

"Deep down, I think the players would have been happy with simply holding our own in the First Division. The management would have none of that, though.

'Winning the Championship, League Cup and European Cup so quickly made us all grow up in soccer sense. Playing in Europe is particularly enjoyable. It's completely different from League football, a real battle of wits.

"If I have any regrets, it's not making a bigger impact with Scotland. I was just coming into the side at the time of the 1978 World Cup. Although I felt I did reasonably well myself, the whole Argentina affair was a disaster for the team.

"It takes time to build up an understanding with different team-mates, knowing how they like to receive the ball and so on. Club calls have restricted my progress, too, but I hope I can make up for lost time."

Those who have seen The Master turning it on for Forest will have little doubt he can.

CAMMY FRASER NEVER LOSES HEART...

There hasn't been an abundance of joy erupting around Tynecastle in recent years to put huge smiles on the faces of the Hearts fans.

The team has hardly touched the dizzy heights the proud club once scaled consistently in the Fifties. Hearts have become a shadow of the line-up that became known as "The Maroon Marauders".

Cammy Fraser, however, has been a player who has come through the worst of it relatively unscathed and he has been one consistent performer within the Tynecastle ranks as they have found difficulty in coming to terms that the Premier Division is really a League that can separate the men from the boys without fuss or argument.

Hearts have found the going too tough twice in succession and flopped headlong into the First Division where they have tried to lick their wounds and fight their way back into the limelight.

Fraser has played away quietly in the midst of the turmoil. There have been no fanatical outbursts of a youngster who might expect football life to be a bit more kind to him.

"It hasn't been easy for anyone," says Fraser. "The fans deserve better,

of course, and every player at Tynecastle is striving to make that possible.

"If you got rewards just by trying hard then things would be looking a lot better. However, that doesn't happen in football. You can't allow frustration to creep into your play . . . that is disastrous."

In the gloom that has descended upon Tynecastle, Fraser has been a shining example to his team-mates. He has never lost his enthusiasm — even when things have obviously been going against Hearts.

One colleague says simple: "Cammy never stops running or trying to encourage you. He gives me the impression

the referee would be putting the whistle in his mouth with us losing 3-0 and he would still be giving his all. That is the type of player he is."

Fraser has been shoved around the Hearts first team in their efforts to plug gaps that have been appearing. He came into the team as a midfielder, had a spell up-front, moved back into the midline, had a go at sweeper and is now back in the middle of the park.

Like a true professional, he says: "I'll play anywhere the boss tells me. I respect his decisions. He has his job to do and I have mine."

The dedication and application from the hard-working Fraser has not gone unnoticed in the transfer market. There was talk last season that Rangers were interested and other clubs, too, had him watched.

His value is obvious. He is a born leader, a young player who readily accepts responsibility. In fact, he thrives on it.

Hearts have been looking for that sort of leadership out on the park for some years now. Cammy Fraser has now given them that.

They must build upon his admirable qualities and make the future a lot brighter for their long-suffering fans.

WHEN I came into international football in 1976, there were many truly top-class players on the scene. the 1974 World Cup had been a good one, with plenty of personalities, while the 1976 European Championship Finals produced football of the highest quality, culminating with that memorable extra-time penalties victory by Czechoslovakia over West Germany.

All the major countries had at least one world-class player, but during the past four years things have changed drastically. Many of the "giants" of world soccer have either retired or gone into semi-retirement in the United States.

I've thought long and hard about this situation, although it is difficult to come up

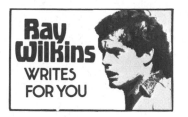

RIGHT . . . "That great character Sepp Maier of West Germany; long shorts, big gloves and lots of personality."

'FEW WORLD-CLASS PLAYERS NOW'

with a reason for the slump. Countries still have a lot of *good* players; indeed, some very good; but in terms of world-class the figure has dropped dramatically since the 70's.

England are lucky to have Kevin Keegan, whom no one would dispute as world-class. Johan Cruyff and Franz Beckenbauer terminated their international careers by moving to the States and it is one of my disappointments that I didn't play against this pair for England. The nearest I came was in 1978 when the Cosmos played Chelsea at Stamford Bridge. Cruyff guested for the Americans and showed just what we were missing during the World Cup Finals that had not long ended.

Even so, I've come up against some extremely talented players during my England career and if my World XI doesn't include many of the true all-time greats . . . it'd still give any side a run for its money!

The best foreign goalkeeper I've played against is SEPP MAIER of West Germany. He's the Continental closest to English goalkeepers in that he always tried to catch centres, while so many foreigners prefer to punch the ball clear.

Maier was a character. Those huge gloves! I've often wondered if they were real!

Sepp played quite a few times against England, but I didn't come up against him until 1978 when we rather unluckily lost 1-2 in Munich. He was outstanding then and I was sorry to hear he was involved in a serious car crash during the summer of

1979 which ended his incredible 13-season ever-present record.

I'll stay with West Germany for my right-back as I don't think there is a classier full-back around than MANNY KALTZ, a team-mate of Kevin Keegan's in Hamburg for three years.

Manny used to be a sweeper, but successfully switched to the right-back berth and became an even better player. There are quite a few full-backs who look good going forward, but their defensive side of the game—which, let's face it, is the more important—suffers. Not so with Kaltz, who knows exactly when to attack and when to hang back. He has marvellous close control for a defender and dribbles in a way that many forwards would be proud to. I remember seeing him score against Wales in the European Championship and since then he has confirmed his status with a high placing in the 1979 European Footballer of the Year poll. Defenders rarely achieve such recognition, but Kaltz's was well deserved.

My centre-back partnership is BRUNO PEZZEY of Austria and DAVID O'LEARY of the Republic of Ireland. I know David plays in the Football League, but Eire claim to be the first foreign side to win at Wembley, so I'm sure I'm correct in calling the Arsenal star a Continental!

I played against Pezzey in the exciting 4-3 defeat in Vienna during the summer of 1978 and the Austria defender quickly took my eye with his cool play. Pezzey is powerful in the air at both ends of the field—England fans won't need reminding that he headed two goals against us,

ABOVE... "Dark-shirted Gentile beats Roberto of Brazil to the ball."

including the winner from a free-kick.

David is similar in many ways. When he breaks from defence, you know trouble is in store. He's very fast . . . those long legs of his seem to eat up the turf and I've never seen the Arsenal man beaten for speed. I believe they say he's the fastest player at Highbury in the sprints, which doesn't surprise me at all.

Left-back I'm going to cheat a little bit, although defenders are becoming more and more adaptable and it's wrong to pin them down to one position. The Italian CLAUDIO GENTILE usually lines-up at right-back, but he has played on the left flank and as he does a man-to-man marking job his role is the same wherever he plays. Gentile looks mean and those who have felt the weight of his tackles will testify that he plays like he looks! Seriously, he may be as hard as nails, but he's fair and is as good a man at his role as you'll find.

I didn't play against the Dutch side that 'slaughtered' England 2-0 at Wembley in 1977; I was in the stands that evening, unfortunately. It must have been an experience to play against a Holland side that was on top form. Had I played against him that night Johan Neeskens, for a start, would be in my team. I can't remember a better all-purpose midfielder than Johan, now with the Cosmos, of course.

Instead, my midfield trio is HERBERT PROHASKA of Austria, FRANK ARNESEN of Denmark and LIAM BRADY, who needs no introduction.

Prohaska reminds me very much of our own Trevor Brooking, one of the highest compliments I could pay him. He goes past defenders like "Hadleigh" (our nickname for the elegant West Ham star) and sets up a lot of chances for his team-mates.

I've played against Denmark twice, in Copenhagen and at Wembley, and on both occasions Arnesen was their best player. He's the nearest I've seen to Neeskens. His pace and strength are incredible—if he were with a more fashionable country he'd be far better known. In Copenhagen, he caused us a lot of problems breaking from midfield, while at Wembley, even though the Danes were, generally speaking, cautious, Arnesen was always looking to go forward.

What more can I say about Liam Brady? You have to talk in superlatives when describing him and while Arsenal have other very good players, any side in the world would miss a player of Brady's ability.

Liam is almost impossible to mark out of a game as he gets away from defenders so easily. Left-sided players invariably have the skill to go past players on the outside—I'm not sure why, but they do—and I've lost count of the times I've seen Liam drift past his marker as if he wasn't there. The answer is not to let him turn, but that is much easier said than done!

When Liam was coming through, he didn't score too many goals. In his last couple of years at Highbury his goal-tally was more in keeping with an attacking midfielder, showing he had matured into a fine all-round player.

I should include Franz Beckenbauer somewhere, but, as I said, I have only played against him in a friendly, never in competitive football. He played in midfield for Cosmos against Chelsea—that's how he started out, moving back to sweeper in the early 70's. Everything Franz did had "class" stamped all over it. It would have been nice to have had a Beckenbauer shirt in my collection.

Regular readers of my SHOOT column will know how highly I rate ALLAN SIMONSEN, the tiny Danish winger. Against England in Copehagen he was superb. Every time he had the ball he created an opening. Allan may be on the small side, but his exceptional speed makes it difficult to flatten him. I also remember the goal he scored for Borussia Mönchengladbach against Liverpool in the 1977 European Cup Final in Rome. Ray Clemence said he has never seen a shot hit harder and I believe him!

If I didn't include Beckenbauer in my team, I'm definitely going to cheat and choose JOHAN CRUYFF! Although the

"Two forwards who are world-class . . . Allan Simonsen and Johan Cruyff."

Chelsea/Cosmos game was a friendly, the Dutch ace took it very seriously as I imagine he does every match. His one-touch football was a delight to watch and the way he opened the Chelsea defence with inch-perfect passes underlined just how sad it was he didn't play in the 1978 World Cup Finals.

I believe Johan could have made the difference between Holland winning and again being runners-up. The competition was crying out for a personality like Johan, although I fully appreciate his decision to quit the international scene.

It was his decision and therefore the right one, even if it did rob us of the chance of seeing one of the most gifted players ever. The pressures on him were enormous—no one can really appreciate this but Johan—and he decided to put his family first, so good luck to him.

Lastly, my left-side attacker . . . ROBERTO BETTEGA of Italy. He's deadly, both on the ground and in the air. He headed a remarkable goal for Italy against England in Rome during a 1978 World Cup qualifying tie and went on to play well during the Finals.

That's it, then, the best "team" I've played against. Maybe in a few years I'll update the side—I wonder how many changes there'll be?

AFRICAN CUP

Played bi-annually, it was introduced in 1957 when only four countries took part. Egypt were the first winners and they have been the most successful country in the tournament's history. Its make-up is similar to the European Championship and World Cup, i.e. qualification followed by Final rounds. Hosts and holders qualify automatically.

ALPINE CUP

A summer competition for clubs in the Alpine region, dominated by those from Switzerland and France.

ANGLO-ITALIAN CUP

Played between invited clubs from England and Italy. In '75 and '76 the participants were both countries' Cup winners.

ANGLO-SCOTTISH CUP

Originally the Texaco Cup, it began in 1971 and was originally open to Irish clubs, also. Generally speaking, clubs who have done quite well, but haven't qualified for Europe, take part.

ARABIAN GULF TOURNAMENT

The major competition for Persian Gulf nations, although Iran, a non-Arab country, hasn't taken part. Started, in 1970, it is played in a host country on a League basis.

ASIAN CUP

Held every Olympiad year since 1956, there are zonal preliminary rounds followed by a Final round contested by the winners. Middle East countries have been reluctant to enter because they refuse to play Israel. Iran have dominated.

BALKAN CUP

Held regularly since 1929 for countries of the Balkan peninsula; it is, in fact, Albania's only national honour to date (1946 winners). Yugoslavia, Greece, Bulgaria, Albania and Rumania are the participants.

BRITISH CHAMPIONSHIP

Needs little introduction. Since it's inauguration in 1884, it has become the showpiece of the domestic season. Used to be played throughout the season, now it is condensed into a week during May. It's the oldest international competition in the world, although the tournament has been dominated by Scotland and England.

CONCACAF CHAMPIONSHIP

Played between members of the Central American CONCACAF nations since 1963, the series has been used to determine qualification for the World Cup.

EUROPEAN CHAMPIONSHIP

Formerly the Nations Cup, or, to give it its correct name the Henri Delaunay Cup, after the former General Secretary of UEFA. Now second only to the World Cup in significance, it began in 1958/60 with the USSR winning; only 17 countries participated. The format has changed slightly, with eight Finalists in Italy this year as opposed to four previously.

West Germany manager Helmut Schoen after his country's 1972 European Nations Cup victory.

EUROPEAN CUP

Played between the Champion clubs of Europe since 1955/56. The early years were dominated by Real Madrid, while the English F.A. blocked Chelsea's entry in the first season, claiming it would interfere with their domestic programme. Celtic became the first British side to win the Cup, in 1967, followed by Manchester United in 1968. Since then, Liverpool and Nottingham Forest (right) have added their names to the winners' list.

Torsten Anderson and Rob Rensenbrink parade the 1977 Cup-Winners' Cup following Anderlecht's triumph.

EUROPEAN CUP-WINNERS' CUP

Started in 1960/61, the competition was not an early success, but has grown in stature since. Open to the winners of the domestic Cups, Spurs were the first British team to find glory, in 1963, with Rangers the first Scottish side to win the Cup in 1972.

INTER-AMERICAN CUP

Contested by the winners of the Libertadores Cup and the winners of the Central American Cup, although not regularly. South American clubs (Libertadores Cup winners) have won every year except one. The Cup is not recognised by FIFA.

OF WORLD

You all know about the World Cup, but around the world there are dozens of other international competitions, both at club and country level, going on virtually all of the time. Here we take a look at many of the Cups that bring countries together—or, in some cases, drive them apart!

INTERCONTINENTAL CUP

Sometimes called the World Club Championship, again, it is not officially recognised. Played, nominally, between the European Cup winners and the Libertadores Cup winners on a home-and-away basis, it has a history of violence and the major European sides are now reluctant to take part. Began in 1960 and Celtic and Manchester United have both been involved in fearsome battles against South American clubs.

INTERTOTO CUP

Little more than a European off-season competition for the benefit of pools companies. There isn't really a winner, just group winners and few of Europe's major clubs take part.

LIBERTADORES CUP

Or, to give it its Spanish title, Copa Libertadores. The most important competition in South America, their equivalent of the European Cup, contested by two representatives from each of the 10 countries. Began in 1960, when Uruguay's Peñarol were the Champions. Played on a home and away basis, the tournament has been the scene of violence and bribery.

LIPTON CUP

Donated by Sir Thomas Lipton, the English tea magnate in 1902, it is played irregularly between Argentina and Uruguay on a one-match basis at alternate venues.

MITROPA CUP

Was the world's first multi-national club competition, launched in 1927. Now, clubs in Central Europe who haven't qualified for the three major Cups take part on a home-and-aways basis.

OSVALDO CRUZ CUP

Played occasionally between Brazil and Paraguay since 1950. Brazil have won every tournament.

ROCA CUP

Dates back to 1914, this Cup has been played for at irregular intervals by Argentina and Brazil.

Aquino of Paraguay displays the South American Cup, December, 1979.

SOUTH AMERICAN CUP

A kind of European Championship, open to all South American nations. It started in 1916, although it is not taken too seriously. Brazil, for instance, often field a State side rather than the national team. Argentina have been the most successful; Paraguay are current Champions.

SUPER CUP

Relatively new (since 1972), the Cup was instigated by the Dutch newspaper *De Telegraaf*. It isn't officially recognised, but has been played regularly between the winners of the European Cup and European Cup Winners' Cup, on a two-leg basis.

UEFA CUP

Formerly the Inter Cities Fairs Cup, the first tournament took three years to complete and was played for by teams representing cities. In 1960/61, qualification was restricted to club sides and in 1966/67 the name was changed to the European Fairs Cup. Leeds were the first British winners and English clubs have dominated the competition (changed to the UEFA Cup in 1971/72) since.

Argentina captain Daniel Passarella with the 1978 World Cup.

WORLD CUP

The world's premier competition, which began in 1930. It has grown in stature over the years and it is not an understatement to say today international football revolves around the World Cup. Brazil have been the most successful country, winning the Cup three times. A total of 47 different nations have reached the Finals, which will comprise 24 sides for the first time in Spain, 1982. England, of course, were Champions in 1966. Brazil are the only country to compete in all 11 World Cup final rounds. There have been 118 Europe/Latin America clashes during the Finals, with Europe winning 50 to Latin America's 46.

DON REVIE was a disciple of dossiers on opposing players when he managed England. Colin Addison, Derby's boss, does not believe in producing manuals for players to digest.

He says: "I have all our immediate opponents checked, but we do not spend long hours with the lads talking about them because we all know the players we will meet.

"After assessing our opponents' current form, collectively and individually, I prefer my players to concentrate on their own play, and the problems they will cause.

'Fat, dumpy' — now City striker

NO matter how talented Football League scouts become, some youngsters always escape the net.

Manchester City's striker Mick Robinson was one whose talents were unrecognised for a long time.

The former Preston North End star was dismissed when a 15-year-old as "a fat, dumpy midfield player."

The story is told by former Blackpool scout Verdi Goodwin, who has unearthed such talent as Tony Waiters, Steve Heighway and Paul Mariner.

Robinson later blossomed into one of the most promising young strikers in the country, tipping the scales at 13 stone and standing six feet tall.

Goodwin grins: "You need a crystal ball in this game."

Alan Ball

IT is hard to believe that the spotlights first fell on football over a century ago.

On October 14th, 1878, the first ever football game to be played under lights was staged at Bramall Lane, Sheffield.

First floodlit game at Wembley was between London and Frankfurt on October 26th, 1955. Wembley's floodlights are 350 feet high and powered by batteries of 1,600 Watt lamps in rectangular reflectors. A might stronger than the average 60 Watt household bulb.

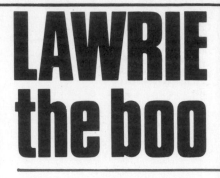

LAWRIE the boo

Manager Lawrie McMenemy condemns those who barrack players from the terraces — and left one fan from the North-East in no doubt about his dislike of the "boo boys".

The confrontation came when Lawrie attended a "question and answer" session in Sunderland.

Lawrie mentioned the barracking Alan Ball had received at Southampton and said he understood that Steve Whitworth had been subjected to the same abuse by a group of Sunderland supporters.

To Lawrie's astonishment a man in the room raised his hand and admitted he was one of Whitworth's most vociferous critics.

Lawrie rounded on him in no uncertain terms snapping: "What gives you the right to abuse people? You wouldn't like it. All you have to think about is whether the player is trying. That's about the only time when spectators can justifiably criticise a player.

NEWS

Compiled by BILL DAY

DESK

Pat's puncture

PAT JENNINGS has become a master at deflating the egos of strikers hoping to plant shots past the Northern Ireland goalkeeper. Imagine Pat's surprise then when he thrust out a massive right hand in a game for Arsenal and deflated the match ball.

Blackpool salute their greats

THE average SHOOT reader will not have had the privilege of watching Stanley Matthews ghosting down the wing for England and Blackpool.

But Blackpool are giving fans a taste of the glory years at Bloomfield Road by creating a shrine to the stars of that era.

Players like Matthews, Stan Mortensen, Bill Perry, Ernie Taylor and others live again in a special showcase opened in the games room at the club.

Fans have contributed old Press cuttings of the vintage years and dusty photographs of that period have been unearthed for the exhibition.

slams boys

"If he's trying, as I'm sure Steve Whitworth is, you're not being fair. You can ruin a player's career and he's got wife and kids just the same as you have."

The questioner came back at Lawrie: "I pay my £1.30 and that gives me a right to say what I like."

"I think the audience were as disgusted as I was," said Lawrie afterwards. "But that incident goes to show that football is outside the normal pattern of behaviour to be found in other jobs when it comes to critical appreciation.

The Southampton manager said that some things said to managers and players were libellous and damaging to the game.

Jimmy Melia, Hugh Fisher and Jim McCalliog, former Saints players, had all been the victims of terrace critics, claimed Lawrie. Alan Ball had been singled out in the 1979-80 season.

Midfield men received more abuse than players in other positions. Alan Mullery and Terry Venables had been given a difficult time by the Tottenham crowd in trying to emulate Danny Blanchflower and Dave Mackay, two midfield stalwarts of the Spurs "double" winning team.

"If fans think a player is a favourite of the manager, they will give him more critical attention. John McGovern found that out at Forest.

"It's wrong to barrack a footballer if he's trying his best."

The 92 Club

WHAT have the manager of a top club, a postman, a chartered accountant, a vicar, a train driver, a tax inspector, a warehouseman, and an auditor in common?

They are all members of the Ninety-Two Club, which recognises fans who have completed visits to all the 92 League grounds for first team fixtures. The club organises trips to selective matches so that the members can get together. Fans who have visited more than 70 grounds and intend to complete a full-house can join.

The Manager is Alan Durban, the young Stoke City boss. He is an honorary member because he had achieved something unique. He had played first team matches in every stadium in the Football League.

A former Welsh international, Alan's playing career spanned all four divisions of the League, with Cardiff City, Derby County and Shrewsbury Town.

His fondest memory? "Season 1969-70 when Dave Mackay had just joined Derby from Spurs and we beat Tottenham 5-0 at the Baseball Ground.

Keith Walker also completed a full-house before he retired from refereeing. He is now involved in North American Soccer.

And a Scotland captain named Gary?

A future captain of Scotland's international team? No doubt about it, Coventry's star defender Gary Gillespie.

Gordon Milne, the Highfield Road boss, is convinced his 6ft 2ins buy from Falkirk will lead out Scotland in the not too distant future.

He captained Falkirk when he was only 17 and is a natural leader.

Where English clubs are lacking — by Tony Book

LIVERPOOL and Nottingham Forest have set Europe alight with superbly competitive football in recent seasons but English soccer still lags behind the Continentals off the pitch.

While Football League teams have won the Champions' Cup, the most prestigous club prize in football, there is a lot of ground to be made up in training and other ancillary facilities.

That's the feeling of Tony Book after a visit to Real Madrid's famous Bernabeu Stadium.

"Every time I travel to the continent, I am inevitably impressed with their organisation so far as sports complexes and facilities are concerned. And they cater not only for football, but for a huge variety of other sports.

"Spain is a prime example. A few years ago Manchester City went to Barcelona and their set-up was absolutely first class.

"Madrid's stadium, for instance, was built at the end of the Second World War; Barcelona's an even more recent project. So why don't we copy?

"For a start I have yet to see an English League ground with sufficient space around it to build anything on the lines these two Spanish giants enjoy.

"What you need is, for example, the Greater Manchester Council to develop the entire Hough End playing field arena and start from scratch by installing gyms, swimming pools, squash and tennis courts, all-weather training pitches, catering areas and everything else that these sort of European organisations have built up over the years.

"Then you start to compete with them in this respect."

SHUTTERED

SUNDERLAND star Claudo Marangoni was involved in an amazing "no goal" incident on his debut for the Roker Park club against Cardiff City in 1979-80.

He powered in a header from a Stan Cummins corner—but the effort was disallowed because an over eager photographer had encroached on the pitch and the flag kick had to be re-taken.

COLIN Cowperthwaite is the new hero of quiz questioners up and down the country.

Few people had heard of Colin before he blasted himself into the record books playing for Barrow against Kettering in an Alliance Premier Division match.

He was credited with the fastest goal ever in football—scored in a staggering 3.55 seconds.

It came from a 55 yard shot. Colin said: "I saw the goalkeeper fiddling about with his gloves and just let fly."

It was the second kick of the match.

Leeds United's John Lukic dives to stop this penalty from Aston Villa's Allan Evans.

SAVED FROM THE SPOT

That's mine! Graham Moseley of Brighton is on the spot to prevent Nottingham Forest's John Robertson scoring.

Bobby (centre) watches a shot by Morton team-mate Andy Ritchie sneak past Partick's Alan Rough.

BOBBY THOMSON
~MORTON'S ACTION MAN

The rival manager took Morton boss Benny Rooney aside and complained bitterly about the Cappielow side's rugged midfielder Bobby Thomson.

The player, a hundred per cent performer who goes in where only the brave tread, had upset this particular manager because of his rightly enthusiastic approach. The following day, however—so the story goes—that same team boss was on the telephone to Rooney asking him to name his price for Thomson!

It may or may not be true, but it is still a perfect illustration of what opponents think of Thomson's power. He is a superb team man, a player who will battle all the way and his type are invaluable in today's game.

"I play football to win", says Thomson, who joined Morton from St. Johnstone in a player-swop deal three years ago. "I go in hard, but I am fair. Football is a man's game, after all.

"You won't catch me moaning if I get hit in a tackle. It's all part and parcel of the game.

"Certainly I like to be known as a competitor. My strength is winning the ball and being able to do something with it. Let's face it, there's not much you can do without the ball, is there? There's no point in the team looking lovely and stylish when we are getting hammered week in, week

Morton manager Benny Rooney admires Bobby's never-say-die qualities.

out. I have a job to do and I try to do it to the best of my ability."

Players such as Billy Bremner, Nobby Stiles, Norman Hunter and Peter Storey in the past and Tom Forsyth, Roy Aitken, Kenny Burns, Jimmy Case and Brian Talbot in the present were and are invaluable to their respective teams because of their grim determination and wonderful spirit. Yet because of that competitive edge they have been on the receiving end of some totally unjust criticism.

"I try not to let it get me down," says Thomson. "After all, I have never set out to harm anyone. When I see a loose ball I want to win it. . . that's my game."

Morton captain Davie Hayes says: "Thomson is so vital to our team, and when things are going against you it is marvellous to see him trying to get things started again.

"He's always in there looking for the ball, shouting for the pass, supporting a team-mate and taking the weight off the defence.

"Really, he is very under-rated, but I know this doesn't upset Bobby. He just keeps on going and Morton continually benefit. Everyone at Cappielow is aware of his true qualities.

"Certainly I would prefer to have him in my team rather than against me. He is a great inspiration to everyone around him. I can't really blame other managers for moaning because of his performances against their sides.

"It can't be easy to pick up two points when a player such as Bobby Thomson is against you."

Thomson may not be as gifted as some of the superstars in today's game, but he still has an awful lot to offer. Mark our words. . .

Ken Hibbitt's right foot was a blur as it hooked the right wing cross deep into Manchester City's net, and one half of the 100,000 Wembley crowd roared in approval.

Wolves were en route to winning the 1974 Football League Cup, but unlike most players who have known the special thrill of scoring at Wembley, Hibbitt discovered that his emotions worked in reverse.

"I remember the rest of the lads celebrating, but all I could think of was how dearly I would have liked my father to have been there to see me," he said.

"He died when I was 17, and if it had not been for my mother's determination I would have stayed at home in Bradford and probably never made it at the top level.

"My brother Terry was already with Leeds United, so when Dad died I decided that my responsibilites were with my mother and sister. I wanted to find out how far I could go in the professional game. But there are priorities in life. And my family had to come first."

Hibbitt's father played a big part in helping the Bradford-born midfield player to shape his career.

"When I left Fairfax School, Bradford at 15, there was talk of joining Terry at Elland Road. But I wanted to go my own way and my father backed me. When I told him that I wanted to work my way up from the bottom he gave me the go-ahead and I joined Bradford Park Avenue.

"It was an incredible experience. I was 15 at the time and could not come to terms with what was happening at Avenue. I reckon about seven managers came and went during my two years there. I played 13 games for them, yet never on a winning side!

"My father's death changed all my plans. But when Wolves showed an interest in me, my mother kept reminding me how much my father had wanted me to make it in the First Division. I argued that he would have wanted me to look after them.

"But she is a determined woman, my mum. And in November, 1968 she virtually pushed me on to a train bound for Wolverhampton. If that train had pulled out five minutes later I honestly believe that I would have grabbed my bags and jumped off. I was still in two minds when the carriage gave a jerk and the train pulled away."

Things did not settle down even then. Wolves signed Hibbitt but days after his arrival, manager Ronnie Allen was sacked.

"He broke the news to the senior players and I was standing in the background listening. I saw their confused and anxious faces and got my first taste of just how unpredictable and cruel this game can be.

"Bill McGarry took over and built a side which I still believe was only two players short of winning the League Championship. In 1971 we finished third in the First Division and the following season stuffed some of the best teams in Europe on our way to the

'Why I began at the bottom' by KEN HIBBITT of Wolves

UEFA Cup Final.

"But of all the teams to play in the Final we had to meet Spurs who, thanks largely to Pat Jennings in goal, pipped us 3-2 over two legs.

"All the time I wanted to really make an impression to justify my family's faith in me. We won the then-popular Texaco Cup, reached the Semi-Finals of the League Cup and F.A. Cup. But always we seemed that fraction short of fulfilling our potential.

"Finally we made it! Wembley in 1974 — the League Cup Final against City. They had the big-name forward line of Summerbee, Bell, Lee, Law and Marsh. But we had the hunger for success after so many near-misses.

"I opened the scoring, Bell equalised and John Richards scored a late winner. It was an unforgettable day in many ways. But I still remember wishing that my father could have seen his wishes fulfilled — Terry and I both playing in the First Division."

Since then Wolves have fallen away to the Second Division, roared straight back, survived two seasons of First Division struggles and emerged as one of the most ambitious and exciting clubs in the League.

Sammy Chung succeeded Bill McGarry, and was in turn succeeded by John Barnwell. He brought in quality players such as Andy Gray, Dave Thomas and Emlyn Hughes. The staff changed rapidly. And since that League Cup Final only five players remain from the victorious 12 — Geoff Palmer, Derek Parkin, John McAlle, John Richards and Kenny Hibbitt.

Settled Now

"There have been times when I considered that a move to a new club would benefit my career. I always wanted to play for England. But one Under-23 cap was all I managed. And I sometimes thought that Wolves ups and downs had not helped my cause.

"But I have been part and parcel of those ups and downs. I like to think that I can take a share of the credit for the things we have achieved. And therefore I must accept my share of the blame for the struggles we have experienced.

"Now I am settled. I suppose I always was. My wife and family live in the area, my friends are here and I believe I play for a club which is genuinely going to make a big mark in the 1980's.

"Our careers are all limited. I have twice suffered injuries which have kept me on the sidelines for months. And one, a broken ankle, came close to ending my career. Once you have gone through that frightening time and come through, you really appreciate every game, every moment and every chance to extend your playing days.

"I count myself among the lucky players. I play for a major club. I have worn the colours of my country, if only once; I have played and scored at Wembley, played in a European Final and been involved in six major Semi-Finals.

"And every time the same thought crossed my mind — the combination of sorrow that my father was not there and gratitude, to him and to my mother, for playing such a big part in helping me to succeed in my career."

They call Graham Rix The Incredible Hulk at Arsenal, a mickey-take of his 10 stone "weakling" frame. The Gunners' midfielder looks like a "before" in a muscle-building advert, but once on the pitch Rix is a giant. . . in talent.

No longer in the shadow of Liam Brady, he is the general of Arsenal's midfield, a star in his own right.

Mind you, during the week Graham doesn't overdo the physical side of training. A few years ago he had a serious back operation, which at one time threatened his career.

He is not allowed to play golf, in case a sudden twist brings back any problems, and weight-training is also out.

"I suppose in a way I save my strength for match-days. I tend to concentrate on things like trapping, passing and shooting during the week."

When Rix was just an apprentice at Highbury, Alan Ball called him "the most promising youngster I've ever seen."

It wasn't long before Graham found soccer has its ups and downs. Arsenal

GOLF IS OUT
FOR GRAHAM RIX

Graham in action for Arsenal against Man. United in the 1979 F.A. Cup Final.

reached the 1978 F.A. Cup Final and Terry Neil had to choose between Graham and Alan Hudson.

"Two days before the game the manager told me of his decision to leave me out. I was the substitute, as Alan Sunderland was fit. He was in, so it was a straight choice between Huddy and me for the vacant spot. Alan got the nod. I was shattered. I felt like packing it all in. I've never been as low."

In fact, Rix played most of the Final as Liam Brady limped off. . . raising question marks about his initial fitness. At the aftermatch inquest, many of the Arsenal players said Graham should have played from the kick-off, some consolation for a losers' medal.

"I learned a lot in that week. Grew up in a way. It taught me to appreciate the good things in the game."

Arsenal were back at Wembley the following year and beat Manchester United in what is known as the Last Gasp Final, with three goals scored in the dying minutes. Rix was chosen from the start—and played well.

"It took me a while to get over the disappointment of that first Final," he says. "I'm definitely a better player for the experience of winning and losing.

"People have suggested I've been inhibited by Liam Brady when we played together. I've always been a fan

Alan Hudson kept Graham out of The Gunners' '78 Final side.

of Chippy, sure, but I felt our styles were different.

"We played on opposite sides of the pitch. I've never been afraid to take responsibility. I enjoy being the play-maker, being involved all the time."

Arsenal coach Don Howe has no doubts about Rix's ability. "I can see him developing into a player similar to Allan Simonsen of Denmark. Graham is deadly accurate with his passing; short distances, over 40 yards or even a delicate chip. What's more, he passes the ball very early and this can split a defence.

"It's overlooked that he also wins a lot of balls with his tackling. Graham can play in midfield, on the wing or up-front. Yes, he's a great little player and could go all the way. . ."

Over to Graham: "I've tried hard to discipline myself. I used to drift in and out of matches. Be involved for ten minutes, then vanish. Football is all about consistency and concentration. Sometimes it's tempting to do the difficult thing, because a tricky pass looks better than a safe one. But the really good players won't give the ball away in such fashion. It's all a question of finding the right balance."

BEFORE the start of every season, Manchester United manager Dave Sexton sets me a target—of at least ten goals. That's the least he expects me to score.

Over the past few seasons I've managed to maintain that average. Not bad for a defender is it?

The boss calls me "Bullet-head" because he says he's never seen a player with as much heading power.

I love scoring goals and would give anything to have a game up front for United. Perhaps I will before I eventually retire.

I suppose you could say I'm a frustrated striker and have to discipline myself to stay back for anything other than set-pieces where most of my goalscoring chances come from.

My presence at free-kicks and corners comes as no surprise to opponents because

'How I've headed for goals glory'

Jackie Charlton caused rival 'keepers many problems during his long career with Leeds.

I've been using my height and strength in the air since my move from St. Mirren to Leeds United.

I learned a great deal at Elland Road from another centre-half who loved scoring goals . . . Jackie Charlton. He was probably the first defender to stand on his opponents' goal-line during corner-kicks.

That tactic was frowned upon at the time, but it's a recognised part of the game now.

My goals record for Leeds wasn't bad. In 140 League matches I scored 15 goals.

The goal I rate as my best-ever at club level was my first for Leeds in a 5-1 win against Sheffield United.

I shall always remember it. I got this header in so hard from a free-kick that when it hit a stanchion at the back of the net it flew out so fast that hardly anyone in the ground realised I had scored.

Play carried on and it wasn't until the referee blew his whistle that fans knew it was a goal.

I'll also never forget two goals I scored for Scotland.

The most vital was the last-minute equaliser against Rumania in a European Championship tie in Bucharest in June, 1975.

Why I'm especially proud of that goal, a right-foot shot from the edge of the area, is because I was captain.

The international goal which has given me most satisfaction to date came a couple of years later against England at Wembley when Scotland won 2-1.

From an Asa Hartford free-kick I headed the ball home from fully 15 yards out. I could have jumped over those famous twin towers when the ball beat Ray Clemence.

Gordon soars above the Arsenal defence to score for United at Old Trafford.

I've scored several memorable goals for Manchester United . . . like the diving header against West Brom in December, 1978.

The ball came across from a free-kick and I simply launched myself into the penalty-area to divert the ball into the net. Unfortunately, United were beaten 5-3 that day.

I also recall the two I scored against Stoke City at Old Trafford on September 29th, 1979.

My first came halfway through the second-half following a corner. Ray Wilkins, who had scored his first goal for United earlier on, floated the ball towards the far post where I was lurking as usual.

I rose above the Stoke defence to score with a thundering header that gave 'keeper Roger Jones no chance.

Then with five minutes of the match remaining, and United well on top, I made the score 4-0.

Our young substitute Tom Sloan centred from the right and I again soared higher than any rival to head home.

I almost made it my first hat-trick but following another header the ball scraped the top of the cross-bar with Jones beaten.

I lived up to my Bullet-head nickname against Nottingham Forest at Old Trafford on 22nd December, 1979.

From a Ray Wilkins free-kick I rifled in a header that Peter Shilton never saw to put United 3-0 ahead.

Joe Jordan had earlier scored twice so United dished out a real treble Scotch to give most of the 55,000 fans a Merry Christmas.

But the United goal I value most was scored against my old club Leeds on my first appearance back at Elland Road following my transfer in February, 1980.

Both Joe Jordan, another ex-Leeds star, and I had received a fair amount of abuse from some of the Elland Road supporters so you can imagine how delighted I was when I headed in after just ten minutes play to put United a goal up. We eventually won 3-2.

Penalty miss

My goal-scoring prowess even tempted me to try my luck as penalty-taker a few seasons ago.

One or two of the regular spot-kickers were out of the side that faced Bolton at Old Trafford during 1978-79.

When United were awarded a penalty I felt confident enough to offer my services.

I scored . . . but the referee, Pat Patridge, ordered me to retake the kick because Joe Jordan had stepped into the area.

Unfortunately, my second shot hit the post and was scrambled clear. I haven't taken a penalty since.

My most embarrassing moment as a goalscorer was captured by the TV cameras and seen by millions of viewers in Scotland.

I was playing for my first professional club St. Mirren against Kilmarnock and determined to create an impression on my debut appearance on the telly.

Then in the second-half Killie were awarded a corner.

As the kick came over I rushed in to boot the ball clear. But at the last minute I hesitated and decided to try and look classy with a placed kick to a team-mate waiting up field.

Instead of finding one of my own men, I

volleyed the ball into my own net from eight yards out.

I certainly wasn't very popular around Love Street that afternoon I can tell you.

At least that own goal taught me a valuable lesson . . . to be positive when making a goalmouth clearance. Never change your mind.

Fortunately I've made amends for that miss-hit during my career South of the border.

Now all strikers will tell you there's no such thing as a bad goal. They all count. But defenders, especially centre-halves, can score flukey goals.

My luckiest goal was scored against Everton at Goodison Park a few years ago.

I was still at Leeds at the time and hit— or rather mis-hit—one of my rare ground shots.

The ball was bouncing about in the Leeds area before landing in front of me. I went to smash it into the net but completely muffed the shot.

Instead of going past the Everton 'keeper like a rocket it sliced off my boot, struck a defender, bounced off a boot and trickled over the line.

Lucky? Sure it was, but proved to be a valuable match-winner.

As a striker on the ground I'm no match for the likes of Joe Jordan. In the air I'd say I'm as good as most strikers.

That side of my game hasn't occurred by accident, though. This is a basic skill which I've concentrated on since a youngster.

Never Hesitate

You have to be brave to go for the ball with your head against several other players with the same object in mind.

You've also got to have timing and confidence. Hesitate going up for a ball and you're dead.

The rest is practice . . . practice . . . practice.

As a lad I spent hours heading a ball against a wall and simply keeping it in the air just using my head.

I would advise any youngster that heading is a vital part of the game and can be improved by following my simple exercises. Practice has certainly paid off for me.

My goalscoring tally over the past few seasons has established me as one of United's recognised strike-force and I get as worried as any of our front-runners if I'm not scoring regularly.

Maybe one day I'll realise my dream and turn out in the number nine shirt for Manchester United.

Until then I'll concentrate on maintaining my unofficial title at Old Trafford—Bullet-head . . . the stopper who scores goals.

All the best . . . join me every fortnight in SHOOT.

Gordon McQueen

One of Gordon's most treasured moments . . . scoring against england at Wembley in May, 1977.

PETER BARNES— W.B.A. and England

'Scored from a kick-off'

Most of my best goals came while I was with Manchester City, certainly the more spectacular efforts. I don't often get my name on the scoresheet, but one I'll always remember came against Bristol City at Maine Road in 1977. They had just scored, and straight from the kick-off I made a run down the left wing. The ball was floated out wide to me, I controlled it first time and then started to go for goal. The Bristol defence were all over the place, and I went straight through four challenges before hitting a low hard shot just inside the far post. We won that one 2-1.

'Robbed by Ray'

My England team-mate Ray Clemence has always been a formidable opponent, and you never get much joy against him. I'll never forget our game against Liverpool just after we had beaten Bristol City, again at Maine Road. It's not often you get a chance to score against the Reds, but on this occasion I received a pass on the right wing and cut in. I thought it was going to be a repeat of my goal a few weeks earlier, especially when I caught the ball just right. It was a low and particularly hard shot but Ray just flung himself across the goal and pushed it round the post for a corner to rob me. I can't remember the final score, but I would imagine Liverpool won.

They usually do!

MICKEY THOMAS—Manchester United and Wales

'My first-time shot almost burst the net'

My best goal was scored for Manchester United against Leeds at Old Trafford in March 1979. Jimmy Nicholl made one of his overlapping runs down the right wing, and crossed the ball deep into the Leeds penalty area. It was headed out, and I was sprinting forward in support of the attack when the ball fell right at my feet 30 yards out from goal. I lashed it first time and it flew past David Harvey into the top corner of the goal. It nearly burst the net.

'Pat astounded me'

The best save I can recall was made by Pat Jennings, typical of the kind of reflex action the Northern Ireland 'keeper has produced over the years. The game was against Arsenal at Old Trafford, and the ball was bouncing all round their penalty area. It came to me about eight yards out from goal and I hit the ball as hard as I could. I was already turning round to claim the goal, when out of the corner of my eye I saw Pat flying to his right. Not only did he reach the shot, he actually managed to hold on to it. I was astounded by his brilliant save, and a crucial one, too, because Arsenal won the game 2-0.

TOMMY CASSIDY—Newcastle United and Northern Ireland

'Unpopular — but I felt terrific'

I don't score all that many, so I usually remember those I do manage. My best goal was scored for Northern Ireland against Scotland at Hampden Park in 1974. There was no score at the time, and the Scottish fans were starting to get a bit worried. I picked the ball up just inside the Scottish half, ran forward and played a one-two. The pass ran just right for me, and I let fly and David Harvey didn't have a chance (pictured here). It turned out to be the only goal of the game, and although I wasn't exactly the most popular guy in Glasgow that night, I felt terrific.

'An equaliser — but for Rankin'

The best save came from former Watford 'keeper Andy Rankin in a League Cup tie at Vicarage Road in 1978. We were losing 2-1 with only a few minutes to go and really piling the pressure on. There was pandemonium in the Watford penalty area as they tried to clear the ball, but it ran right to my feet at the edge of the box. I just hit through a mass of players hoping that it would take a deflection.

It went straight through a Watford defender's legs, but somehow Rankin managed to spot the ball as it came through the ruck and got down to turn it away. But for him, it would have been the equaliser.

MICKY WALSH—
Queens Park Rangers and Eire

"Goal of the Season" winner'

I suppose a lot of people could tell you my best goal. It won BBC "Match of the Day's" 'Goal of the Season Award' in 1975. It was while I was still with Blackpool in the Second Division against Sunderland at Bloomfield Road. We were under pressure from the Sunderland forwards when Paul Hart cleared the ball out of defence up to me on the half way line. I took the ball on my chest, cut in past two defenders and hit a shot from about 30 yards into the top corner of the net.

'Billy never gave up...'

It's hard to classify the best save, because the spectacular ones are not necesarily the best. One great save came when I was playing for Everton against Ipswich at Goodison Park. Andy King chipped the ball over their defence and I ran on and chested it down. I hit a shot on the half-volley, but Paul Cooper flung himself across and made a tremendous save.

Another time I thought I was certain of a goal in the 1979-80 season when Q.P.R. beat Burnley 7-0. It was an amazing game, with poor Billy O'Rourke making his debut in the Burnley goal. He had played really well, but his defence gave him absolutely no cover, and we were just walking the ball into the net.

We were already 7-0 up when I gained possession on the left. I played a quick 1-2 with David McCreery and then shot for the far corner. I was convinced it was going in, but O'Rourke dived full-length and tipped it around the post. It was a great save made even better because at that stage nobody could have blamed the lad for being demoralised. But he never gave up and showed great spirit to make that save.

IAN WALLACE—
Coventry City and Scotland

'My perfect overhead kick'

I'll never forget the goal I scored against Norwich at Highfield Road at Christmas 1977. It came in an incredible game which Coventry won 5-4, and my goal was the second. We won a corner on the left, and Tommy Hutchison touched it short to Barry Powell. The Norwich defence rushed out to catch us offside and I had to come away from the goal-line to keep up with them. Barry crossed the ball, and I was standing around the penalty spot with my back to goal. The ball was about five feet off the ground, and I instinctively took off and tried an overhead kick. I caught it perfectly, and Kevin Keelan was just rooted to the spot as my effort flew in just under the bar. It was the kind of goal Denis Law used to specialise in, and I was particularly pleased with it, because Denis used to be my hero.

'Best save I've ever seen'

As for the best save a 'keeper has ever made from one of my shots, my mind is a blank. I never remember the saves, just the goals! The best save I can recall seeing was during the England v Scotland game at Wembley in 1979. Scotland were a goal up when Kenny Dalglish chipped a shot to the far corner. Ray Clemence had already started to move for it, when Dave Watson tried to head it clear but only deflected it to the other side of the goal.

It looked an own goal all the way, and the Scottish fans were already up on their feet. But Ray somehow managed to twist in mid-air, and just managed to touch it over the bar for a corner. If that one had gone in, I'm sure Scotland would have won the game, but soon after England equalised and went on to win 3-1.

IT'S AMAZING how over the past few seasons we've virtually seen the end of the so-called superstars. . . the individuals, the soccer heroes capable of adding thousands to gates wherever they played.

I'm talking about the likes of Bobby Charlton, Denis Law, Bobby Moore, Gordon Banks and Jimmy Greaves. And before them John Charles, Tom Finney, Stan Matthews, Len Shackleton, Jackie Milburn and Raich Carter.

Not so long ago clubs such as Manchester United, Everton, Arsenal, Spurs, Derby County and West Ham were packed with top names.

Ask any fan 15 years or so ago to name the Spurs side and it's a good bet he knew every player. That certainly wouldn't be the case today.

Somebody asked me recently to run through the Chelsea team. . .and I could only name four.

As a nipper I remember being given a clip around the ear by my teacher because instead of paying attention to what she was saying I was writing down the names of the Manchester United team.

You see I was a United fanatic as a kid—still am in a way— and knew them all. . .Pat Crerand, Denis Law, David Herd, Pat Dunne, Shay Brennan, Alex

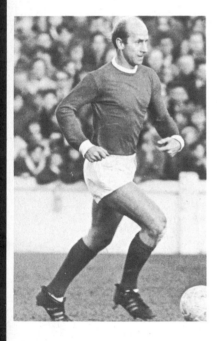

Stepney, David Sadler, Bobby Charlton, John Connolly and George Best.

George Best is still capable of pulling in large crowds, of course, as he proved at Hibernian.

The wayward genius was perhaps the first of the modern superstars, the man responsible for opening the commercial doors for the rest of us.

Many of today's top players certainly owe George a debt of gratitude.

There are still many great players around these days, of course, but few with the same magnetism of a Best, Moore, Charlton or Greaves. So where have all the heroes gone?

The game's changing. The days of the individuals are almost over. Today leading clubs place the emphasis more on team

MY SOCCER WORLD
Viv Anderson

'MANAGERS ARE TODAY'S BIG NAMES'

Left: Bobby Charlton during his glory days with Manchester United.
Right: Jimmy Greaves . . . a real soccer hero of the not too distant past.

work. Players aren't really given an opportunity of displaying the full range of their skills.

Defences are better organised. . . . defenders have to be all-rounders, capable of setting up attacks as well as stopping them.

I wonder if old stars such as Stan Matthews and Jimmy Greaves would be so successful today. I doubt defenders would allow them the room to operate.

You don't often see today's forwards go off on mazy dribbles, beating five or six men before driving home from the edge of the box.

And Jimmy Greaves wouldn't get so many chances inside the penalty area.

Sure, we still have players capable of turning it on during a match. . .stars such as Stan Bowles, Tony Currie and Trevor Francis, but they often have to stifle their natural flair for the good of the team.

A few years ago a players of Bowles' skill and class would have been an England regular, instead of an international outcast.

Today players are becoming more and more anonymous. Ask fans who they know from Ipswich and the majority will plump for Bobby Robson.

It would be the same at places such as Manchester City (Malcolm Allison), Norwich (John Bond), Chelsea (Geoff Hurst), Aston Villa (Ron Saunders), Crystal Palace (Terry Venables), Brighton (Alan Mullery), Southampton (Lawrie

McMenemy), Watford (Graham Taylor, or probably Elton John).

That's right, so many of today's soccer headline-makers are the managers, not the players.

Lack of real personalities on the field, the characters of the game, may well be one reason for falling gates.

Fans will always pack Anfield and Old Trafford, but Liverpool and Manchester United are exceptions. There the clubs are the drawing power. It doesn't really matter who wears the red of Liverpool or red and white of United.

The number of footballers people will travel miles to see are down to a handful.

As I've already said, George Best is still capable of pulling in crowds. After joining Hibernian last season their gates trebled. So did other attendances in the

Scottish Premier Division.

Nottingham Forest are fortunate. I reckon we have three super stars who attract fans wherever they play. . .Peter Shilton, Trevor Francis and Stan Bowles.

Then, there's Andy Gray at Wolves, Kenny Dalglish at Liverpool. . .Liam Brady at Arsenal, and Ossie Ardiles at Spurs.

There may well be a shortage of players with personality plus but we've still an abundance of first class experienced players and emerging youngsters to ensure the future of the game.

Forest have one lad destined for the very top, 19-year-old Gary Mills.

Manager Brian Clough rarely goes out of his way to praise a youngster for fear of ruining him. All he usually says

*Left: Ipswich boss
Bobby Robson, the
club's top personality.*

when asked about a particular lad making his way up the ladder is: "He's okay. He'll make a living"

Some kids start believing their own publicity and it goes to their heads. When they fail to live up to great expectations they can't cope and drift out of the game.

No such fears with midfielder Gary. He was just 16 and fresh out of school when the boss picked him as substitute for Forest's vital European Cup-tie against AEK Athens during the 1978-79 season.

At the time Mr. Clough said he had no worries about sending him on in such a cauldron of a match.

"I'm not going to wrap him up in cotton wool," I remember him saying to a reporter. "Mills has the ability to stand on his own feet, even at his age."

Gary stood up for himself all right and is now an important part of Forest's future plans.

Mind you, it's not surprising Gary is making his name in football. His dad Roly Mills was a Northampton player for almost 20 years and is still at the club as commercial manager.

Gary tells me he was something of an all-round sportsman at school. He played soccer and rugby for England and ran in two Championships.

A brilliant youngster already living the lifestyle of a soccer superstar is Bristol City midfielder Kevin Mabbutt.

He lives in a luxury flat in the stockbroker belt of Bristol drives an expensive sports car and has a self-promotion company

CONTINUED
OVERLEAF

CONTINUED

Kevin's younger brother Gary, who plays for Bristol Rovers, could become an even bigger name in football.

Last season he skippered the England Youth team and was described by manager John Cartwright as "the most exciting youngster in the country".

Leicester manager Jock Wallace is also sure he's picked a winner in mid-fielder Andy Peake.

I've seen him in action several times and was impressed with his vision and confidence. He's only around 18-years-of age yet never seems flustered no matter who he's playing against.

Apparently Andy has styled himself on his boyhood hero David Nish, the Leicester and Derby defender. Like David I'm sure he'll go on and become an England international star

Tommy Caton could also make the full England side in the near future. The Manchester City youngster was plunged into the first team by Malcolm Allision when he was barely 16.

I understand Tommy could have joined Liverpool the club he supported at school but chose City because he felt he stood a better chance of making progress.

That chance of big-time soccer came a lot sooner that this big centre-half imagined, when Dave Watson moved to Werder Bremen in West Germany during the summer of 1979.

Big Mal had no hesitation in handing this former Youth international with seven ' O'' levels Dave's number five shirt.

My other tips for stardom in the

Above: Leicester midfield man Andy Peake (dark shirt) an England international star of the future. Left: So is Manchester City defender Tommy Caton.

1980's. . .Coventry's central-defender Garry Gillespie, who became the youngest captain ever known in British professional football when he was made skipper of Falkirk at 17.

Now 20, this giant stopper has established himself in the heart of Coventry's defence and looks a great prospect for club and Scotland. maybe as a future captain.

Vince Hilaire is already something of a crowd-puller because of his all-action style.

He's a joy to watch on the ball one of the best balanced players in the country. Few can match Hilaire's control.

Leeds United's tiny terror in attack Terry Connor is also well on the way to making a valuable contribution to the game as a character and personality.

This boy wonder was an instant hit when he came into Leeds first team last season. The goal he scored against Arsenal at Highbury in January 1980 was a real gem. . and had even the ardent Gunners fans applauding.

Terry brushed aside Steve Watford, fastened on to a Paul Madeley pass and drove the ball hard and low past Pat Jennings.

More goals like that from youngsters will soon draw the fans in. I d pay just to watch him!

All the best, join me again in SHOOT some time.

'WHAT THE FUTURE COULD BRING...'

Everyone loves to do a bit of crystal ball gazing, trying to guess just what the future holds. But the great fascination of football is that it defies prediction.

For example back in 1960 who could have foretold what the next 20 years were going to bring in world football? How many Englishmen would have predicted a World Cup win for England in front of their own fans?

How many Celtic supporters in those days when the European Cup was a Real Madrid monopoly, would have put hard cash on their idols becoming the first British club to win the tournament?

Who could have predicted that there would come a team so good as the 1970 Brazil World Cup side or players so good as Cruyff, Dalglish, Best or Keegan........ or that Pele would become even better?

And perhaps the most unpredictable thing of the 20 years following 1960 was that a footballer would be transferred for £1,500,000.....and I write that in full deliberately because I still cannot believe the size of the fee Wolves paid for Andy Gray.

After all, back in '60 little Andy had still to start school and was hardly big enough to kick a ball at all.

So now that I have convinced myself how difficult it is to predict anything in football—especially over a period of two decades—I am going to do just that.

Prepare yourself for the McGrain version of football at the turn of the century!

Well, right away I will say that I won't be surprised if Andy's transfer record is still standing at the end of the century. Transfer fees are beyond a joke now and I think clubs are waking up to this fact.

Kevin Keegan paved the way for players to negotiate their own transfer fees when he settled with Hamburg and Southampton and told them what they could sell him for at the end of his contract.

And besides, I think only Kenny Dalglish in Britain would command a fee in excess of Andy's price.

But what else lies ahead? Well, 20 years, even 40 years ago, they were talking about a British League and we are no nearer it now than we ever were.

Perhaps it will happen before the new century dawns.....but I doubt it. To be honest there is little for the English clubs to gain although some of the old arguments against it don't count any more.

In this jet set age clubs should think nothing of flying from Southampton to Aberdeen. And that jet argument could be just the key to real possibility in the future......a European league.

Just imagine Celtic v Juventus or Anderlecht v Rangers as part of your weekly football menu. Mind you, it could become a bit expensive being a member of a supporters' club!

One thing I don't think will change

Danny believes transfer fees have peaked. Only Kenny Dalglish (below) is likely to realise more than record fee holder Andy Gray.

Tartan Talk
DANNY McGRAIN

over the next two decades is the continuing exodus of Scottish players to England and indeed what would happen to English football if the trafficking did halt?

Scottish players have been the life and blood of the football League since its inception and unfortunately I don't see that altering.

Freedom of contract will be with us of course, but it is very difficult to predict what will happen there. So I won't!

The sad truth is that I can foresee more clubs both north and south of the border doing a Third Lanark and folding completely. By the year 2000 Scotland may have only two leagues and the Second Division will be full of part-time teams.

It is almost inevitable that the big clubs are going to get bigger and the small clubs smaller. It is a sad state of affairs, but that is the way the cookie is crumbling.

I don't think we will ever again see a monopoly of the European Cup in the way Real Madrid controlled it at the end of the Fifties. I thought Liverpool were real kings but they could only hold it for two years and it is

asking too much of any team in the world in these competitive times to do what Real did.

The future for Scotland looks bright such is the form of our Under-21 side, as long as the lads realise that it is a big jump to the full team.

However, I don't think things are as bright for the future of soccer in America as some people would have us believe. In my opinion the acceleration has eased off and I honestly don't think they will become a power in world football for a long, long time yet.

So that is the way I see it. Some of my ideas could be way off the mark and indeed in some of the things I have said, I hope they are. But the big thing about the greatest sport in the world is that it stimulates discussion.

Everyone loves a football argument. Including us players!

THE CRYSTAL PALACE STORY

The Palace revival began in 1976 when Terry Venables replaced Malcolm Allison as manager.

At the end of his first season in charge the club won promotion from the Third Division behind Mansfield and Brighton.

Two years later they were Second Division Champions and then for a few brief weeks early last season The Eagles sat proudly perched on top of the League — above the Liverpools and Manchester Uniteds.

Malcolm Allison promoted The Eagles nickname which was probably first used by fans when the club played at a ground called The Nest just after the Second World War.

Their first home was at the old Crystal Palace, where the early F.A. Cup Finals were played.

In 1915, Palace moved to Herne Hill and four years later to The Nest at Selhurst.

Then in 1922 the club bought some land from a railway company at Selhurst Park and they've been there ever since.

Crystal Palace were formed in 1905 when Mr. W. G. McGregor, founder of the Football League, asked Mr. E. F. Goodman of Aston Villa to help form a new club.

Mr. Goodman not only helped but provided the team with a complete playing kit in the claret and blue of his beloved Villa.

Palace were elected to the Second Division of the Southern League and won the title and promotion at their first attempt.

But Palace's history didn't really

Left: Terry Venables . . . looking to the future. Right: The team that shot to the top of the First Division at the start of the 1979-80 season.

THE EAGLES

WHEN Crystal Palace hammered Ipswich Town 4—1 at Selhurst Park on September 29th, 1979 to go top of the First Division, a few weeks after taking promotion, their brilliant young manager Terry Venables remarked: "Liverpool may well have been the team of the Seventies but we could be the team of the Eighties."

True, The Eagles soon came down to earth, their wings clipped later by the likes of Liverpool, but the fact they were able to reach such heights justified Venables' ambitions and positive attitude.

Whatever Palace achieve in the Eighties, they'll do well to match the remarkable success of the late 1970's.

The decade began with the club in the First Division for the first time in their history, and ended with them coming back for another attempt to not only establish themselves, but become one of the country's leading clubs.

In between there were two relegations, a promotion, Second Division Championship and an F.A. Cup Semi-Final appearance.

John McCormack (partly hidden by a post) scores a vital goal against Ispwich in March, 1972. That gave Palace a priceless point and helped them to avoid relegation to the Second Division.

kick-off until 1920 when the Football League decided to extend their Third Division and elected the entire First Division of the Southern League.

They did fairly well in the Third Division (South) just failing to win promotion in 1930-31 and 1938-39.

Their most famous player during that period was Peter Simpson who scored 154 goals in 180 League appearances, still a club record.

Albert Dawes, whose brother Fred later managed the club, was another Palace star of the 1930's.

The Second World War brough a halt to League football in Britain, of course, but not Palace's transfer dealings.

The club signed so many players during the War years they had to appeal to supporters for lodgings and clothing coupons for playing kit.

Palace hardly set South London alight when hostilites ended. The best position they achieved was seventh in the Third Division in 1949-50, under manager Ronnie Rooks . . . their third boss since the war.

After Rooks' sacking he was replaced

HAVE LANDED

by joint managers Fred Dawes and Charlie Slade, rather like the Clough-Taylor combination of today.

Unlike Clough and Taylor, though, the Palace pair didn't find success and three times in seven years the club had to seek re-election.

Former Arsenal and England defender Laurie Scott was next in the Selhurst Park hot-seat, followed within a year by Cyril Spiers, the ex-Aston Villa, Spurs and Wolves goalkeeper.

But they had another disastrous season and in 1957-58 dropped into the newly-formed Fourth Division.

George Smith, a strict disciplinarian, took over from Spiers, but even his harsh measures failed to lift the team.

Two years later he resigned. Arthur Rowe, creator of the push-and-run style which made him a legend as manager of Tottenham, moved in and immediately won Palace promotion, when they finished the 1960-61 season behind Peterborough.

Just beforehand, Palace had made another significant signing, Margaret Montaque, the first woman secretary of a Football League club.

Palace were on their way up, guided by Rowe and the skill and flair of a 17-year old centre-forward named Johnny Byrne.

April, 1969 and Palace fans celebrate victory over Fulham and promotion to the First Division for the first time.

The slender little forward scored 32 goals and won two England Under-23 caps in Palace's promotion season.

He became the first Third Division player to gain full England honours when he replaced Jimmy Greaves against Northern Ireland in 1962.

The ending of the maximum wage added to Palace's mounting financial problems, forcing them into selling Byrne to West Ham for a then-record fee of £65,000.

Rowe didn't handle the transfer though; he was ill at the time. The club was in the hands of assistant-manager Dick Graham.

But the team didn't like Graham's tough training methods and protested to the club's directors demanding his dismissal.

The ultimatum was rejected. The board stood by Graham who promptly began to sell off the dissidents.

Half the side went, including Byrne and Bill Glazier, sold to Coventry for £35,000. a then-record fee for a goalkeeper.

The new signings, Cliff Holton, Ronnie Allen, Brian Whitehouse, Bert Howe and Brian Wood—most of whom

CONTINUED OVER

had been with Graham at West Brom helped Palace to promotion in 1963-64.

Success didn't mellow Dick Graham. He still proved a difficult man to understand.

He upset the Press and rival managers by refusing to name his team until the last minute. Then he would send out his players wearing "wrong" shirts. The right-back would be wearing number ten, the number three would appear on the right-wing.

It was because of his action the Football League introduced the rule making it compulsory for managers to announce their line-ups half-an-hour before kick-off.

In January, 1966, Graham was sensationally sacked after another series of blow-ups in the Palace dressing-room.

Arthur Rowe returned as general-manager; and coach George Petchey, whom Graham had sacked a week earlier, was appointed acting-manager.

Three months later, Palace gave the job to Bert Head who arrived from Bury having previously had great success with Swindon.

In his third season, in 1968-69, Head took Palace into the First Division for the first time in their history with a team full of experience. . .players such as Mark

Lazarus, Bobby Woodruff, Cliff Jackson, and a young 'keeper named John Jackson.

But Palace hardly made progress in the First and finished 20th in 1969-70 and 18th in 1970-71. Bert Head, famous for discovering young talent at Swindon, decided the club needed fresh blood.

Out went Steve Kember to Chelsea for £170,000, Alan Birchenall to Leicester for £100,000 and Phil Hoadley to Orient for £30,000.

In came John Craven, Bobby Kellard, Bobby Bell, John Hughes and Willie Wallace.

These new faces failed to lift Palace and they ended 1971-72 in 20th place again.

As they plunged towards relegation in 1972-73 Bert Head moved upstairs to become general-manager and Malcolm Allison arrived in a blaze of publicity to take over the team.

He came smoking large cigars, drinking champagne and making promises. . .but he couldn't save Palace from going down into the Second Division.

Worse was to follow when in 1973-74

One of today's Palace stars Billy Gilbert in action against Ipswich.

Above: 1975-76 F.A. Cup Semi-Final v. Southampton at Stamford Bridge. Palace lost 2-0 . . . and here David Peach scores for Saints from the penalty-spot. Left: Mike Flanagan, a big money buy.

the club slumped even further, to the Third Division.

The Eagles finished 1974-75 in fifth position and didn't really take off under Allison until 1975-76.

They began in great style, losing only once in their first 20 games and led the Third Division table by Christmas.

Promotion seemed a certainty until at the turn of the New Year things started to go dramatically wrong.

Palace won only one of their next 12 games, and Allison fell foul of famous illusionist Romark, who put a curse on the Palace manager.

The club failed to go up and even lost to Southampton in the F.A. Cup Semi-Finals.

Allison's reign at Selhurst Park was ended, but at least he can claim some credit for the success that subsequently came to the club for while in charge he had appointed Terry Venables as coach.

Venables, then just 33, took over as boss during the summer of 1976 and led Palace back to the Second Division in his first season.

Two years later he was celebrating a Second Division Championship triumph.

Before accepting the Palace job, Venables had turned down an offer to take over as Arsenal manager. He also later rejected a one million dollar bid by Cosmos of New York in favour of a four year contract with Crystal Palace.

And what of the future? As Terry himself has said: "I can't see myself spending the rest of my career at Palace. I feel I will need a new challenge at the end of my four years."

Then he may well become the new manager of England, in succession to Ron Greenwood.

Until that time, though, Palace can look forward to continued progress.

The team is full of talent. . .Vince Hilaire, Ken Sansom, Jim Cannon, John Burridge, Jerry Murphy, plus the experience of former England skipper Gerry Francis, and the power up front of £750,000 signing from Charlton Mike Flanagan.

Signs are that Crystal Palace are well prepared to fulfil Terry Venables' hopes and ambitions for the Eighties.

It's a Football Fact — MANAGERS

Quick-change Q.P.R.

Queens Park Rangers once had as many as four different managers in less than three months! In November 1968 General Manager Alec Stock resigned and left team-manager Bill Dodgin jnr. in charge. Within a couple of days Tommy Docherty was appointed manager with Bill Dodgin as his assistant. However, after just one month Docherty resigned and player Les Allen acted as caretaker before being officially given the job of manager on January 8th, 1969.

Bossed eight clubs—and Scotland

Nobody ever had a more wide-ranging experience of club management in the Football League than the former Preston North End and Scottish international full-back, Andy Beattie. His managerial career began with Barrow soon after World War Two. In 1949 he moved to Stockport County, from where he took over at Huddersfield in April 1952. Subsequently he managed Carlisle United (1958-60), Nottingham Forest (1960-63), Plymouth Argyle (1963-64), Wolverhampton Wanderers (1964-65), and Notts County (1967). Apart from these eight clubs and a number of different jobs with other clubs he was also Scotland's team manager for a spell in 1954 and again in 1959-60.

Much-travelled

Another much-travelled manager was the famous Major Frank Buckley who earned such a reputation in the 1930s for developing youthful soccer talent. A centre-half with Aston Villa, Brighton, Manchester United, Manchester City, Birmingham, Derby County, and Bradford City before World War I, his first managerial post was with Norwich City in March 1919. Subsequently he managed Blackpool, Wolverhampton Wanderers, Notts County, Leeds United, and Walsall, before finally retiring at the age of 71 in June 1955.

First four-figure salary

Which was the first Football League club to pay their manager a four-figure salary? Arsenal? Manchester United? Liverpool? No, it was none of these powerful clubs. It was Middlesbrough, a club that has yet to win the League Championship. The man in question, Scotsman, Peter McWilliam, had won three Championship medals and an F.A. Cup medal (as well as three Cup finalists medals) as a wing-half with Newcastle United. At the end of his playing career he became manager of Tottenham Hotspur before taking over at Middlesbrough in January 1927.

Rare player-managers

You won't find many player-managers transferred to another club in the same capacity. In December 1951 the former England international centre-forward, Freddie Steele, was transferred from Mansfield Town, where he had been player-manager for two-and-a-half years, to Port Vale, where he continued as player-manager until the end of season 1952-53 when he finally hung up his boots and remained as manager until January 1957. Indeed, he returned for a second spell as Port Vale's manager 1962-65.

Considering the number of times the majority of clubs change their managers it is worth noting that West Ham United have had only five in the 80 years of their existence. The first was Syd King who remained in charge until 1931 when he retired and was succeeded by the club's trainer, Charlie Paynter, who, incidentally served West Ham in various capacities for 50 years. When he retired in 1950 his assistant, Ted Fenton, took over. Ron Greenwood was Fenton's successor in 1961, and after a spell as team-manager John Lyall took over in 1977.

How many Football League club player-managers have appeared in the British Championship? The answer is two. Most fans will know that Terry Neill is one of them, making six appearances for N. Ireland in the Championship during just over four years in charge of Hull City and before moving to Tottenham Hotspur in September, 1974, but how many can recall the other player-manager who played for this country? He was Stanley Davies, an outstanding inside-forward in the Football League during the 1920s when he was with Preston North End, Everton and West Bromwich Albion. On one of those unfortunate occasions when the Welsh F.A. were placed in an almost impossible position with so many Football League players being withdrawn from their international side, they were forced to recall Stanley Davies after an absence of nearly two years This was for the game against Ireland in Belfast in February 1930 at a time when Davies was rounding off his playing career as player-manager of Rotherham United in the Third Division (North). It was a sad finale to his international career for the much-weakened Welsh side were thrashed 7-0 with Linfield centre-forward Joe Bambridge scoring six goals in succession.

Terry Neill, player-manager of Northern Ireland, scores against England at Wembley in 1972.

MATCHES THAT MADE HEADLINES

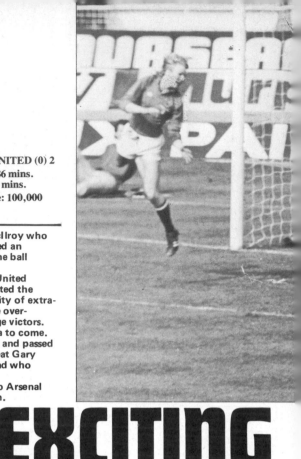

1979 F.A. Cup Final—Wembley

ARSENAL (2) 3	v.	MAN. UNITED (0) 2
Talbot 12 mins.		McQueen 86 mins.
Stapleton 44 mins.		McIlroy 88 mins.
Sunderland 89 mins.		Attendance: 100,000
Receipts: £500,000		

NOT since 1953 when Stan Matthews won the F.A. Cup for Blackpool in that famous see-saw affair against Bolton had Wembley witnessed such a nail-biting finish to the world's most glamorous club competition.

Three goals in four minutes rescued this 1979 Final. Until then it had hardly been the showpiece this meeting of the giants had promised.

Although the game will always be remembered for its sensational, almost bizarre climax, it was also a personal triumph for Arsenal's Republic of Ireland international midfielder Liam Brady.

Coppell's pass reached McIlroy who beat two men and side-stepped an advancing Jennings to slide the ball home.

Wembley erupted as the United players and their fans celebrated the equaliser . . . and the possibility of extra-time when they would be the over-whelming favourites to emerge victors.

But there was more drama to come. Brady dribbled down the left and passed to Graham Rix. His centre beat Gary Bailey and reached Sunderland who slammed in the winner.

So F.A. Cup glory went to Arsenal for a superb grandstand finish.

THE MOST EXCITING

Wembley was a fitting stage for this elegant performer who played a leading role in each of Arsenal's goals.

In the 12th minute he produced a crossfield run which tore the heart out of United. Three opponents were left floundering before a perfect pass found Frank Stapleton, who drove the ball hard and low into a crowded penalty-area.

Alan Sunderland and Brian Talbot went for it together, but the former Ipswich star got the final touch to send the ball into the roof of the net.

Soon after United had their chance to pull level, but Mickey Thomas struck a Sammy McIlroy pass straight at Pat Jennings.

Then a Joe Jordan header skimmed the crossbar and Jimmy Greenhof saw his spectacular effort fly inches too high.

Just as the Royal Marine band appeared at the tunnel entrance to pre-pare for their half-time entertainment, Arsenal scored a second goal.

Brady, the ball sticking to his boot as if by magic, beat two defenders and crossed to the far post where an un-marked Stapleton had the compara-tively easy task of heading into the net.

United offered little but token resistance after the interval. A Lou Macari effort apart they rarely troubled an Arsenal side coasting to victory . . . until the 86th minute.

Then Steve Coppell's long floated free-kick was knocked on by Joe Jordan and Gordon McQueen swept the ball in.

No one in the United team seemed particularly interested in the goal which at the time appeared a consolation. But that attitude was to change a minute or so later.

AFTER MATCH QUOTES
ARSENAL

Manager Terry Neill. (right)
'Now we've won the F.A. Cup I want to say that I don't want this to be a one-off affair. This is just the start.'

Brian Talbot, who collected his second successive winner's medal with different teams. 'We felt we let them come back from two goals down and had thrown it away when our winner showed our character. Physically it was harder than last year's Final, but it was never dirty. It was nice of Prince Charles to say "Well played Brian" when I collected my medal.'

Liam Brady, who made all three goals. 'I was dreading extra time. I was out on my feet and we had already brought on the sub.'

Brian Talbot (number 4) gives Arsenal the lead in the 12th minute.

LEFT . . . Almost unbelievably, Alan Sunderland (number 8) wins the Cup for Arsenal with this last-gasp effort.
RIGHT . . . Gordon McQueen salutes his goal that signified United's dramatic comeback.
BELOW . . . United manager Dave Sexton felt United deserved a replay.

...FINISH EVER?

Man-of-the match Liam Brady didn't give his Wembley medal away after this Final. The previous season, against Ipswich, he handed his loser's medal to his friend, Arsenal kit-manager Tony Donnelly, known in the game as "Golden Studs".

LEFT . . . Man of the Match, Liam Brady.
ABOVE . . . Sammy McIlroy (left) is about to score United's equaliser, but it wasn't enough to stop Arsenal.

The teams . . . and how they rated

Arsenal	Man. United
Jennings 8	Bailey 8
Rice 7	Nicholl 6
O'Leary 8	McQueen 7
Young 7	Buchan 6
Nelson 7	Albiston 6
Price (withdrawn) 7	Coppell 6
Talbot 8	McIlroy 6
BRADY 9	MACARI 8
Rix 8	Thomas 7
Sunderland 7	J. Greenhoff 6
Stapleton 8	Jordan 6
Sub. Walford	

Referee: Ron Challis 9

HOW THEY REACHED WEMBLEY

ARSENAL
THIRD ROUND:
Sheffield Wed. 1 v. Arsenal 1 (Sunderland)
replay: Arsenal 1 (Brady) v. Sheff. Wed. 1
second replay: Sheff. Wed. 2 v. Arsenal 2 (Brady, Sunderland)
third replay: Arsenal 3 (Stapleton 2, Young) v. Sheff. Wed. 3
fourth replay: Sheff. Wed. 0 v. Arsenal 2 (Gatting, Stapleton).
FOURTH ROUND:
Arsenal 2 (Young, Talbot) v. Notts County 0
FIFTH ROUND:
Nottingham Forest 0 v. Arsenal 1 (Stapleton)
SIXTH ROUND:
Southampton 1 v. Arsenal 1 (Price)
replay: Arsenal 2 (Sunderland 2) v. Southampton 0
SEMI-FINAL:
Wolves 0 v. Arsenal 2 (Stapleton, Sunderland)

MAN. UNITED
THIRD ROUND:
Man. Utd. 3 (Coppell, Grimes, J. Greenhoff) v. Chelsea 0
FOURTH ROUND:
Fulham 1 v. Man. Utd. 1 (J. Greenhoff)
replay: Man. Utd. 1 (J. Greenhoff) v. Fulham 0
FIFTH ROUND:
Colchester 0 v. Man. Utd. 1 (J. Greenhoff)
SIXTH ROUND:
Tottenham 1 v. Man. Utd. 1 (Thomas)
replay: Man. Utd. 2 (Jordan, McIlroy) v. Tottenham 0
SEMI-FINAL:
Liverpool 2 v. Man. Utd. 2 (Jordan, B. Greenhoff)
replay: Man. Utd. 1 (J. Greenhoff) v. Liverpool 0

MR. VERSATALITY WANTS TO SETTLE DOWN

It shouldn't surprise anyone to learn that if the Leeds United goalkeeper was injured during a game, Brian Greenhoff would be the man to take over between the sticks.

Greenhoff even played in goal for Manchester United, against Birmingham, and he tells with some pride that "it was 0-0 when I took over and we ended up winning 2-0."

Brian's versatility is an asset to his manager, but in many ways it has worked against him as he hasn't really been able to establish himself in any particular role.

He began as a forward or a midfielder; moved to the centre of defence; then to full-back. Wherever he plays, Greenhoff plays well, yet he says: "It's nice to be able to slot in anywhere. It gives me more options. On the other hand I want to settle down to a midfield role.

"Leeds seem to prefer me in this position and it suits me fine. I think most midfielders could play at the back, though. It's even easier at international level. There have been quite a few midfielders who have become sweepers and vice versa."

Greenhoff has dropped out of the international scene after three years and 17 caps, 13 of which were won under Don Revie. Injuries at unfortunate times and the continued impressive form of that other man-for-all-positions Mick Mills have gone against the Leeds man.

Luck hasn't been too kind to Brian, who has had, among other injuries, a broken leg.

Six years after his debut for Manchester United, he moved on to Leeds United; the writing was on the wall when he was only the sub for the 1979 FA Cup Final against Arsenal. Incidentally, that was his fourth Cup Final. He has two losers medals and one winners' — he was also a ball-boy for the 1968 League Cup Final at Wembley.

It cost Leeds £325,000 for the 27-year-old international and, surprisingly, the decision to leave Old Trafford wasn't as difficult as you'd imagine.

"I was born in Barnsley and used to watch Leeds when my brother, Jimmy, played for them. I enjoyed my career with United — let's face it, they're the biggest club in the world.

"Having said that, the facilities at Elland Road are every bit as good. We had some rare old tussles when I was with United against Leeds. Jimmy Adamson is doing a good job getting a 'new' side together after the hey-days of the Seventies. I'm enjoying my football every bit as much as I did in Manchester."

It was ironic that as Brian was leaving Old Trafford, brother Jimmy was sidelined with a pelvic injury that threatened his career.

The brothers remain very close and Brian, seven years the junior, says: "I always thought Jimmy should have had more recognition.

"We didn't play together much as kids because of the age difference. When he joined United I came to appreciate his skills. I've yet to see anyone who lays off a first-time pass as quickly or accurately as Jimmy. He also made himself available and if you were in trouble, nine times out of ten Jimmy would be there to help out."

Brian prefers to look to the future, but inevitably, as is the case with everyone who has played for Manchester United, a bit of Old Trafford goes with them.

"I made my debut in September, 1973, at Ipswich and stayed in the side for the rest of the season.

"I should be at my peak right now and I'm confident I can win more honours with Leeds.

"Last season we had a lot of injuries and team-changes and it was hard to get going. Even so, youngsters such as David Connor and John Lukic made a name for themselves which augurs well.

"I haven't given up hope of an international recall. Ron Greenwood knows my best position . . ."

112

FASTEST

Sendings-Off

Ambrose Brown of Wrexham was sent off after only 20 seconds of a Third Division III (North) game at Hull on Christmas Day 1936.

Billy Rankin was sent off when making his debut for Charlton Athletic v. Port Vale, March 19th. 1932. Other players sent off in their first game for a new club include George Whitelaw (Halifax Town) 1959, George Casey (Torquay United) 1967, and Brian Myton (Middlesbrough) 1968.

Flying Goals Start

Look through the list of record goal-scorers for the Football League clubs and you will find that centre-forward Ted Harper still holds the record for two clubs - Blackburn Rovers (43 goals in 1925-26) and Preston North End (37 goals in 1932-33). Before Jimmy Greaves broke it by one, with 37 goals in 1962-63, Harper also held the record for Tottenham Hotspur with 36 goals in 1930-31. In his best season of 1925-26 he got off to a flying start with 14 goals in his first seven appearances. This included five in one game at Newcastle.

Own-Goals

The fastest "own goal" in the Football League was that scored by Alan Mullery (Fulham) for Sheffield Wednesday on January 21st 1961. Fulham kicked-off and Mullery put the ball into his own net when trying to pass back to his goalkeeper. Sheffield Wednesday had taken the lead without any of their players touching the ball.

Former Everton full-back Tommy Wright had the unenviable record of two fast "own goals" on consecutive Saturdays! He scored one for Liverpool in 33 seconds on March 4th, 1972, and the following week scored another "own goal" in only 32 seconds when playing Manchester City.

The fastest "own goal" in an F.A. Cup tie was that scored by David Fretwell (Bradford City). He put Luton Town one up after only 20 seconds from the kick off in a fourth round tie on January 26th, 1974.

Two Goals in 90 Secs

Frank Worthington scored two goals in only 90 seconds for Leicester City v Leeds United. Division 1, April 20th 1976. Leicester won 2-1.

FRANK WORTHINGTON

The fastest goal ever scored in a home international was that netted within 10 seconds of the start by Edgar Chadwick (Everton) when playing for England against Scotland, at Ibrox Park, April 2nd, 1892. England went on to win 4-1.

When Plymouth Argyle met Rochdale in a Third Division game at Home Park October 11th, 1969, three goals were scored in the first four minutes. Trevor Shepherd got one in only 20 seconds for the Argyle, but then Dennis Butler netted two for Rochdale in the space of two minutes and the visitors went on to win 3-2.

Peter Kitchen was fast off the mark with Doncaster Rovers in 1970-71. When making his debut for the club at Shrewsbury he scored in only 90 seconds. The following week, in his home debut against Swansea City, he got the ball into the net after only 95 seconds.

Hugh McIlmoyle scored in all four Division of the Football League within a period of only 16 months. On April 25th, 1963, he netted his last Fourth Division goal for Carlisle United. The next season he scored for them in the Third Division before being transferred to Wolverhampton Wanderers and scoring in Division One. Wolves were relegated that season and McIlmoyle scored for them against Coventry in the Second Division on August 21st 1964.

Super Century

The fastest century of goals in the Football League was that scored by West Bromich Albion's record-breaking centre-forward, Jimmy Cookson. Here was a player to delight the hearts of the majority of fans who like to see the ball hitting the back of the net. He began his professional career as a full-back with Manchester City but had no success. Moving to Chesterfield in 1925 he switched to the attack and was an immediate success, scoring 86 goals for them in two seasons before West Bromwich Albion snapped him up. In his first season with them he reached his century of goals in only his 87th game, a record which is unlikely ever to be equalled. By the time he retired in 1939 this fine player had scored 256 League goals in 292 games, including further goals with Plymouth Argyle and Swindon Town.

Bert Turner (dark shirt) who scored for both sides in the 1946 FA Cup Final.

Scored for Both Sides

Bert Turner, the Charlton Athletic half-back, is generally credited with scoring for both sides in a match in the shortest time. This was in the 1946 Cup Final when he put Derby County ahead with the first goal after 81 minutes, turning the ball into his own net, but then almost immediately equalised by sending a free-kick crashing through a crowd of defenders and into the Derby net. However, Derby won 4-1 in extra time.

ALLAN EVANS
Aston Villa

114

RAY KENNEDY
Liverpool

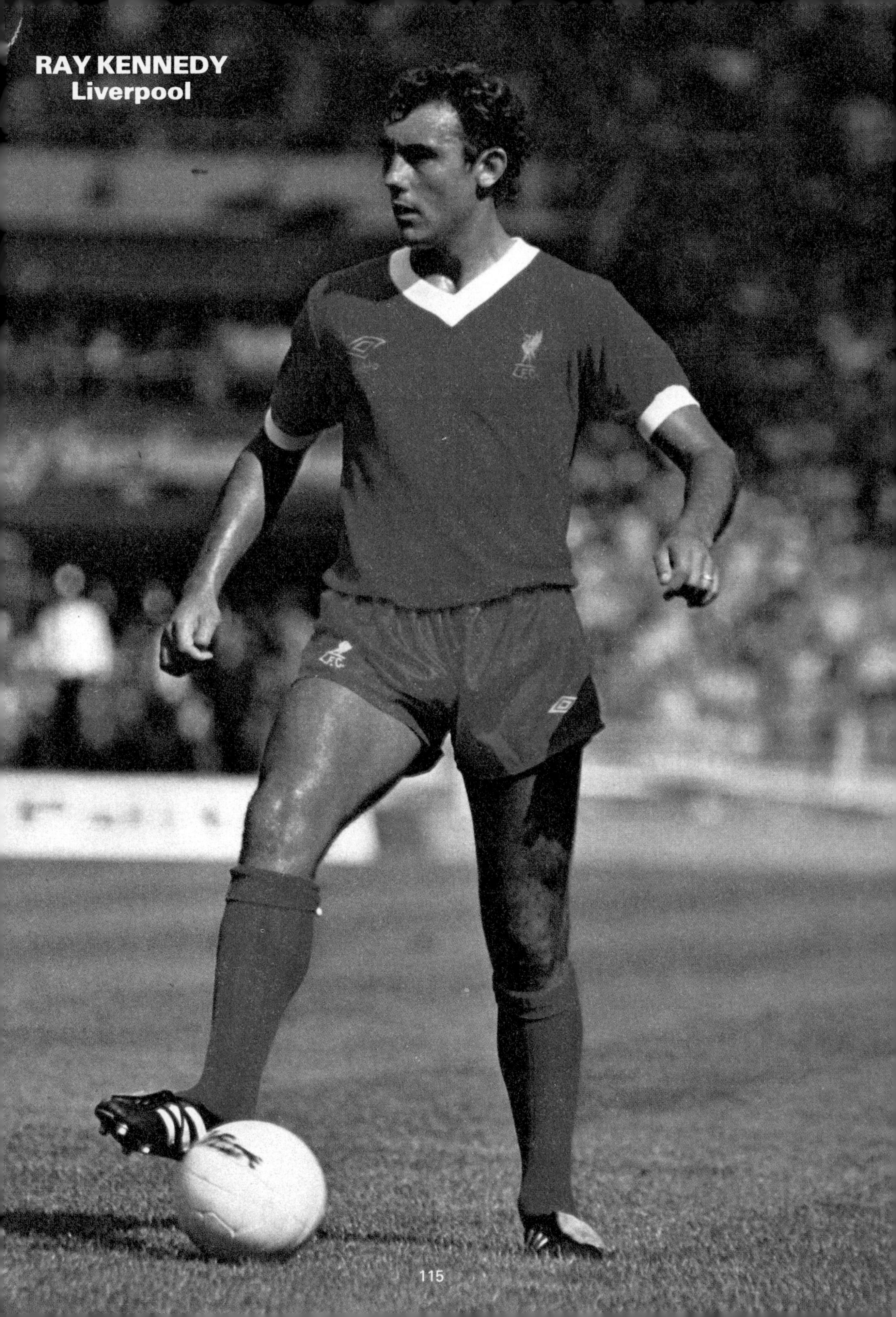

Last season there was a very interesting and intriguing poll organised between the managers of the Top Ten clubs in Scotland.

They were given the opportunity to select a side from all the teams other than their own. Some of the choices raised eyebrows and some were fairly predictable.

Billy McNeill (Celtic), John Greig (Rangers), Bertie Auld (Partick Thistle), Davie Sneddon (Kilmarnock), Tommy Gemmell (Dundee), Jim Clunie (St Mirren) and Benny Rooney (Morton) had no hesitation in naming the players they would like to see operating on the right hand side of their midfield.

They all went for Aberdeen's mighty atom Gordon Strachan, a player who, at one stage in his career, was thought of as too hot to handle!

"I got a bit of a reputation for being a bad boy," says the Pittodrie stylist. "I was getting into trouble with referees because of my quick temper and not doing myself any good at all.

"I got sent off in a reserve game while playing for Dundee against Dundee United in rather strange circumstances. United had a set of twins in their team that day and one of them fouled me from behind.

"When I turned around they were both standing together, so I didn't know which one was the culprit. What did I do? I went for both of them! The referee had little option but to send me off. See what I mean about having a quick temper..."

That temper has been firmly in control, however, since his £80,000 move from Dens Park to Aberdeen four years ago.

Realising that it was a mug's game to continually argue with referees and

'MIGHTY ATOM' GORDON

THE MANAGERS' CHOICE

query their decisions, Strachan decided to put his flashing talents on display for all the world to see.

"I knew I had ability," he says, "and I knew it was time that it was consistently proved to the fans. While I was a reserve player with Dundee I picked up the 'Young Reserve Player of the Year' twice in succession. That might not mean much, but the award comes from nominations from rival managers so it shows that they thought something of me."

And after that poll last year they still do! Strachan's form in recent years has been a real eye-opener. He has paraded the midfield, winning the ball, picking up loose passes, making himself available and delivering breathtaking long-range through balls into the heart of enemy territory with the accuracy that Franz Beckenbauer at his best would be proud to claim.

There have been disappointments along the road, though. Strachan returned to Dens Park with Aberdeen last season for the League Cup Final replay against Dundee United and everyone thought it was going to be a slaughter. The game on Saturday had been drawn and Aberdeen were so much on top that someone observed at the final whistle: "Aberdeen annihilated United 0-0!"

And there was a slaughter at Dens Park . . . with The Dons collapsing to an astonishing 3-0 defeat. It was hard to take for the players who had done so well to knock out the Big Two of Celtic and Rangers on their way to the Final.

There can be little doubt that Strachan's time will surely come. A player of his outstanding talents deserves success and honours. The flaming temper has gone, he is maturing with every performance and he could easily become another Billy Bremner for the Scottish side in the near future.

He certainly has the talent and the ability. There can be no question about that.

FOOTBALL is all about partnerships. There are some double-acts that come together and click with magnificent results. In the last World Cup Finals in Argentina there was the marvellous pairing of Mario Kempes and Leopoldo Luque, the spearhead that took the South Americans to the global crown.

There was Puskas and di Stefano in the great Real Madrid side and there have been many other pairings whose styles have moulded and fused into one. Some people call it telepathy, but footballers tend to scoff at it.

One double-act that rarely hit the headlines was one at Partick Thistle that broke up last year when both players, Bobby Houston and Doug Somner, left Firhill for new clubs. Houston is now with Kilmarnock while Somner has gone to St. Mirren.

Here we give the players the opportunity to talk about their new lives apart . . .

Doug Somner (stripes) jumps high.

When a double-act splits up...

HOUSTON: I remember that well. I was happy and sad at the same time. Happy because you obviously knew your own mind and were delighted to make the move, and sad because I was losing a good colleague and team-mate, on and off the field.

SOMNER: It wasn't long before you, too, were packing up and leaving Firhill. What happened there?

HOUSTON: It was no secret. Things weren't quite working out the way I expected with Thistle and I was happy to leave. I didn't know whether I was part of the manager's plans or not and it was a bit unsettling. When Kilmarnock came in and offered Ian Jardine in a swop deal I couldn't sign on the dotted line quick enough.

SOMNER: I often think back to those days at Firhill, Bobby, and wonder if we'll ever team-up again.

HOUSTON: Like you said earlier, Doug, you can never take anything for granted in this game and everything is possible. Anyway, keep knocking those ball into the net . . . just so long as it is not against Kilmarnock.

SOMNER: And you keep swinging over those brilliant crosses from the right wing . . . but not against St Mirren.

'You must be missing my magnificent service' — Bobby Houston (now Kilmarnock)

Bobby Houston (stripes) stretches for the ball.

'I wonder if we'll ever team-up again'— Doug Somner (St. Mirren)

HOUSTON: I suppose you must be missing all those magnificent high crosses I used to send over for you to knock into the net.

SOMNER: You mean, of course, those dangerous mishits that I had to throw myself at in an effort to direct them towards the opponents' goal?

HOUSTON: You're joking, of course. Your memory must be failing you, Doug. The way I remember it, you just stood around the goalmouth and I hit the ball off your head into the net!

SOMNER: Yes, I am joking . . . but so are you! Seriously, though, I suppose we did have a good partnership with Partick Thistle. It certainly brought me a fair amount of goals.

HOUSTON: Yes, I keep telling everyone that I made you a £100,000 star because of my magnificent service!

SOMNER: I did score a couple of goals on my own initiative, you know. . .

HOUSTON: Yes, but those were scrappy affairs. Nothing like the spectacular efforts I set up. Honestly, though, I thought we would both end our playing days at Firhill. Did you?

SOMNER: Well, I believe you can never take anything for granted in football. I started my career with Falkirk before going on to Ayr. I thought was settled there before I went to Thistle in a swop deal. However, I suppose I was still a bit surprised when I learned of St Mirren's interest in me.

HOUSTON: They had just sold Frank McGarvey to Liverpool, hadn't they? They were looking for another proven goalscorer.

SOMNER: That's right and I'm just thankful that manager Jim Clunie decided to take a chance on yours truly. Actually, Bobby, once the transfer went through and there were no hitches, you were one of the first people I 'phoned with the news.

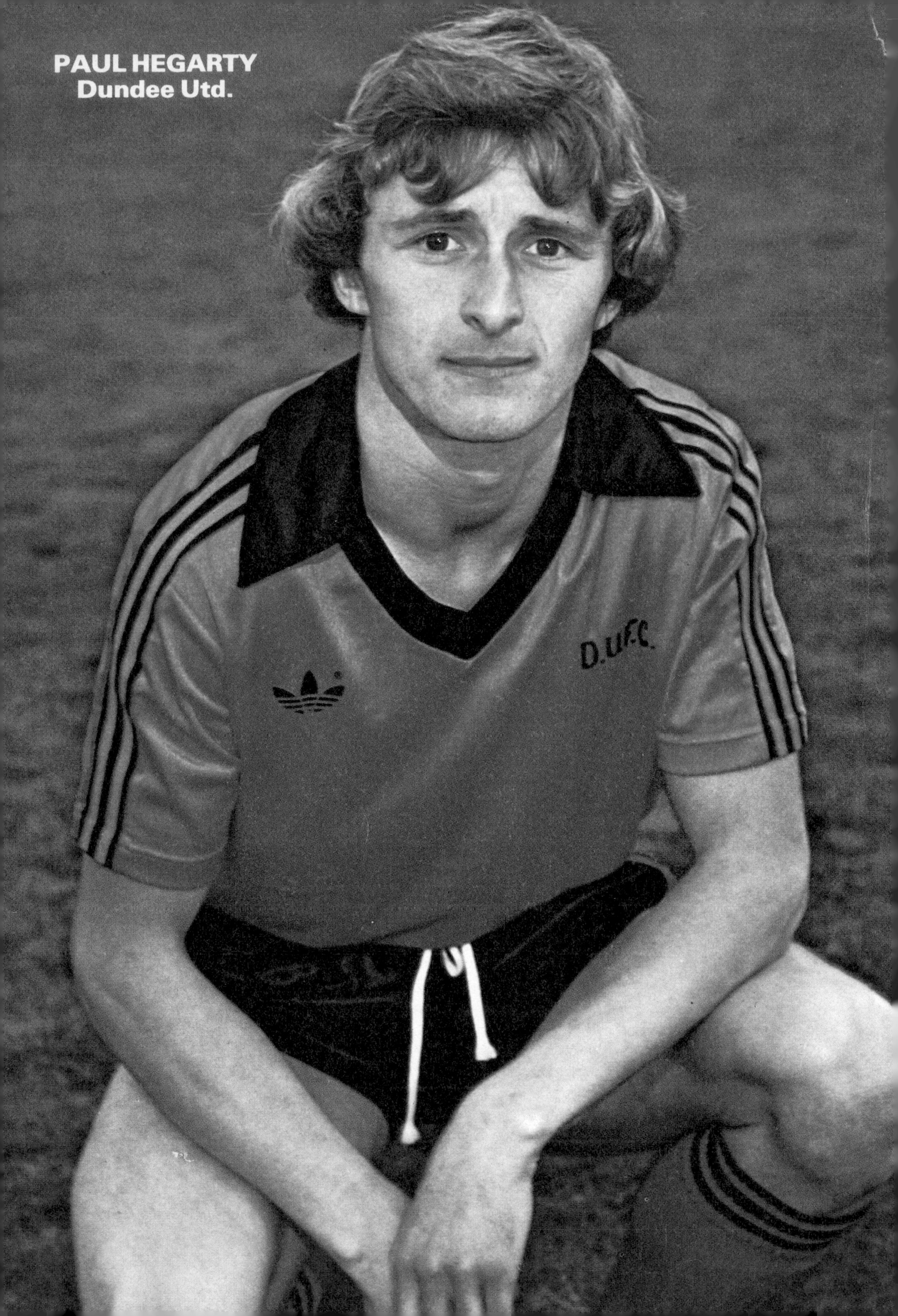

PAUL HEGARTY
Dundee Utd.

Ipswich Town's Terry Butcher (left) and Alan Brazil team-up against Middlesbrough.

MATCHES THAT HIT THE HEADLINES

1978-79 European Cup Final
NOTTINGHAM FOREST v.
MALMO
Olympic Stadium, Munich,
May 30th, 1979
attendance: 57,500

King Francis wins crown for Forest

Trevor Francis, Britain's first £1 million footballer when moving from Birmingham City to Nottingham Forest in February, 1979, repaid a sizeable chunk of that fee in the Olympic Stadium, Munich.

Francis, making his first European Cup appearance in the Final against the Swedish Champions Malmo, capped a magnificent first-half display with a goal moments before half-time.

His header proved enough to defeat Bob Houghton's team of part-timers to keep the European Cup in England for the third season in succession.

The England forward gave a five star performance in a Forest side missing Archie Gemmill and Martin O'Neill.

Forest used the skills of Francis on the right side of midfield where he was ably aided by that most versatile of super-substitutes Ian Bowyer.

Twice Francis raced through the Swedish defence only to see his perfectly judged passes wasted by team-mates.

Then Bowyer struck a tremendous long ball through to Francis who quickly passed to the overlapping Viv Anderson.

The defender's cross was hit first-time by John Robertson, but was deflected behind by Roland Andersson.

There was no denying Forest's superiority. Malmo seemed content to keep the score down and stopping Forest displaying the flourish and flair with which Brian Clough wanted to succeed Liverpool as European Champions.

Forest's constant pressure left them exposed at times and in the 40th minute Kindvall broke through and sent over a cross which eluded Peter Shilton.

Fortunately for Forest, and the relief of their 20,000 fans in the stadium, there was no other Malmo player far enough forward to take advantage of the cross.

Then seconds before half-time Forest got the goal they deserved.

Bowyer started the move with a pass to Robertson. The Scottish winger beat two men before crossing the ball to the far post, where Trevor Francis, after a 30-yard dash, was on hand to head home.

With skipper John McGovern magnificent in midfield, John Robertson causing havoc on the flanks, and Trevor Francis completely in command on the right, Forest continued to dominate after the interval.

But Malmo defended defiantly and the two Anderssons, Erlandsson and Jonsson, cleared when it seemed Forest were about to add to their score.

Then John McGovern sent a long ball out to Trevor Francis. He took it to the byline and pulled it back across the area

Trevor Francis dives to head home against Malmo.

to Robertson, who promptly drove the ball against a post, with 'keeper Moller hopelessly out of position.

No one in the Olympic Stadium, and the watching millions on TV denied Forest their crown . . . but they would have cheered that victory even louder had Malmo contributed more than just boring, defensive tactics to this Final.

Teams:

FOREST: Shilton; Anderson, Lloyd, Burns, Clark, Francis, McGovern, Bowyer, Robertson, Woodcock, Birtles.

MALMO: Moller; Roland Andersson, Jonsson, Magnus Andersson, Erlandsson, Tapper (Malmberg), Ljungberg, Prytz, Kindvall, Hansson (Tommy Andersson), Cervin.

Nottingham Forest— Champions of Europe.

HOW THE FINALISTS GOT TO MUNICH

First Round *first leg*
FOREST 2
(Birtles, Barrett) v. Liverpool 0
MALMO 0 v. Monaco 0
Second leg
Liverpool 0 v. FOREST 0
Monaco 0 v. MALMO 1
(Kindvall)

Second Round
first leg
AEK Athens 1
(Mavros) v.
FOREST 2
(McGovern, Birtles)
Dynamo Kiev 0 v. MALMO 0
second leg
FOREST 5
(Needham, Woodcock, Anderson, Birtles 2) v.
AEK Athens 1
(Bajevic)
MALMO 2
(Kindvall, Cervin) v.
Dynamo Kiev 0

Quarter-Finals
first leg
FOREST 4
(Birtles, Robertson pen, Gemmill, Lloyd) v.
Grasshoppers 1
(Silser)
Wisla Krakow 2
(Nawalka, Kmiecik) v.
MALMO 1
(Hansson)
second leg
Grasshoppers 1
(Sulser, pen) v.
FOREST 1
(O'Neill)
MALMO 4
(Ljungberg 3, 2 pens, Cervin) v.
Wisla Krakow 1
(Kmiecik)

Semi-Finals
first leg
FOREST 3
(Birtles, Bowyer, Robertson) v.
Cologne 3
(Van Cool, Dieter Muller, Okudera)
Austria WAC 0 v. MALMO 0
second leg
Cologne 0 v. FOREST 1
(Bowyer)
MALMO 1
(Hansson) v.
Austria WAC 0

MATCH STATS

Forest:			
	Shots On Target	Off Target	Fouls
Anderson	0	1	6
McGovern	0	2	1
Lloyd	0	1	1
Burns	0	0	2
Francis	1	1	1
Bowyer	1	0	2
Birtles	0	2	1
Woodcock	1	1	3
Robertson	1	1	2
Totals	4	9	19

Malmo:			
Andersson.R	0	1	1
Erlandsson	0	0	3
Jonsson	0	1	2
Andersson.M	0	0	1
Ljungberg	0	2	6
Prytz	0	1	0
Hansson	0	0	3
Cervin	0	0	1
Kindvall	1	0	1
Malmberg	0	0	1
Totals	1	5	19

Corners: Forest 8. Malmo 3
Offside: Forest 21. Malmo 7

AFTER-MATCH QUOTES:

Brian Clough (Forest manager)
"We are worthy successors to Liverpool as European Champions. As far as my career is concerned this is a marvellous milestone, but it doesn't mean as much as winning the First Division Championship. The first time we did that at Derby was the highlight of my life and nothing will surpass it."

Bob Houghton, Malmo's English manager:
"They were the better side, technically and in terms of skill. They are worthy Champions of Europe. If a Forest player had to win the game I'm pleased it was Trevor Francis. He must have been under enormous pressure since being bought for £1 million."

Bob Paisley, Liverpool manager.
"I'm happy for Forest and Brian Clough. It is a tremendous achievement and I am pleased the trophy is staying in England. With them succeeding us as European Champions, you can say fair exchange is no robbery."

Clough and Taylor show the strain.

West Brom striker Ally Brown leaps high against Liverpool.

BILLY ASHCROFT
Middlesbrough

Liverpool were once "also rans". During their early years The Reds showed little consistency, flitting between the First and Second Division and were overshadowed by their Everton neighbours. Then in 1905 they began an unbroken run of 49 years in the top section and rightly joined the ranks of Football League "greats". But in 1954 very dark clouds descended over Anfield when they ended the season at the foot of the First Division with only 9 wins in their 42 games, and were relegated. The next few seasons were a struggle and there was little for the Kopites to cheer. Then in 1961 Liverpool appointed Bill Shankly as manager and at the end of the season the Reds were Division Two Champions. From then on the sun shone again over Anfield as the club rose from mediocrity to magnificence and in the years that have followed have justly earned the title of "the greatest club in Britain."

It might have been so different. . . . If Everton had not refused to pay an increased rental to the landlord of Anfield in 1882 there might have been no Liverpool F.C. But when The Blues found a new home at Goodison Park the landlord of the Anfield ground decided to start his own football club in 1892 and application was made for membership of the Football League. It was turned down flat! However, the newly founded Liverpool club were determined to succeed and in 1893 were elected to the Second Division. The climb to greatness had begun. . . . . .

In 1892 Nottingham Forest were elected to membership of the Football League, four years after their local rivals, Notts County, had become founder members. But although Forest won the Cup in 1896 it was to be a long time before they joined the "Soccer greats". Between 1906 and 1922, they spent only one season in the upper class, the rest of that 16 year period was in the Second Division. In 1915 they returned to Division Two where they remained until 1949. Then an even greater tragedy struck the club. They dropped into the Southern Section of Division Three. After two seasons they regained a position in the Division above where

they struggled along until 1957. Although they won the Cup in 1959, from 1972 until 1977 they were "Second raters" but then the miracle happened, a miracle that owed much to the inspiration and leadership of Brian Clough and Peter Taylor.

Winning the League Championship in 1978 — the first title in the club's long career, two League Cup triumphs in 1978 and '79 and the European Cup also in 1979, Nottingham Forest achieved greatness. It had been a long time coming but no one can deny that they have earned their membership of the elite.

Leeds United also left it late before being elected to a place among the super clubs. They began in 1920 as members of the Second Division, but from then until 1964 they led a see-saw existence. Every few years they switched from First to Second Divisions and vice versa but never enjoying any sustained success. In 1962 they narrowly escaped relegation to Division Three.

Drastic measures were needed to save the club from disaster and the man chosen to lead the club's fight-back was 34 year-

When today's top

There is no prize for naming Britain's great clubs. No one would deny that clubs like Liverpool, Arsenal, Nottingham Forest, Spurs, Manchester's United and City, and several more according to your own personal fancy, are worthy of the proud title of "Great". But much of the real greatness of some of these clubs has been built up over recent seasons— at least since the War. If we delve back into past history we find they weren't ALWAYS great.

Leeds' skipper Billy Bremner with the UEFA Cup.

BILL SHANKLY

of the top honours too, but greatness wasn't earned without a few ups and downs, especially in their early days. Incidentally, Spurs first met their present neighbours in 1888 on a roped-off pitch in a local park near Tottenham and beat them, although, of course, their opposition were called Royal Arsenal from Woolwich. They were elected to the League, Division Two in 1893. Spurs had to wait until 1908, even though they were Southern League Champions in 1900 and FA Cup winners a year later.

The Lilywhites soon became a very popular London club but Arsenal faced problems. Across the Thames at Woolwich The Gunners failed to attract much support. Eventually, in 1913, they took over a disused school sports field at Highbury, North London. Before they could settle in they were relegated to the Second Division with a dismal record of only 18 points (3 wins, 12 draws) to finish at the bottom of Division One. Strangely enough, two years later Spurs followed them into the lower section.

Even after the war no one could claim that the two North London clubs

might have disappeared from the Soccer scene. A move to Old Trafford in 1910 began a run of success that ended when the first World War put an end to football.

Then from 1919 until the Second War United did little to enhance their fame, suffering relegation three times. But in 1945, without a home of their own as Old Trafford had been badly damaged by Nazi bombers, Matt Busby became the club's manager. There is no need to enumerate all United's successes during the years that followed, culminating wtih their triumph in the 1968 European Cup Final, the first English club to achieve the honour.

Aston Villa's entry into the ranks of the really great clubs came early in their career. Original members of the Football League in 1888 they remained in the top class for 50 unbroken years, during which time they were six times Champions and six times Cup winners. Their fame and glory lasted until 1967 when the clouds gathered over Villa Park, and they were relegated to Division Two. But worse was to follow. In 1970 they dropped into the Third, a tragedy for the once great Midlands club. Since

clubs were also-rans...

old Don Revie, United's captain and former Manchester City FA Cup winner. To state that Don worked wonders would be putting the matter mildly. From the position of Division Two Champions in 1964 Leeds became a power in the game, winning all the top honours in League Championships and Cups, including the UEFA Cup twice, led by that tiny, red-headed dynamo Billy Bremner. There was no finer team in Britain during the reign of Revie and Bremner, a reign that put Leeds United into the Football history books as one of the "Greats" better late than never!

North London is the home of two of the undisputed finest. Arsenal and Spurs, of course. Both clubs have enjoyed fame for a good many years and a goodly share

Manchester United's Bill Foulkes and Bobby Charlton parade the European Cup.

were worthy of rank among the great clubs. Yet, as we all know, the '50s and '60s saw the old rivals matching each other for the big honours — and a place in Soccer's Hall of Fame.

Few of the really great clubs have not suffered set backs to knock some of the shine off their fame. It happened to Manchester United who, during their early years in the League, nearly went bankrupt and but for the generosity of a local business man of wealth, who paid off the club's substantial debts,

then Villa have regained some of the lost ground but it will be a long and hard struggle before the shine returns to their once proud Roll or Honour.

Wolves had a somewhat chequered career before they achieved real fame and glory. It's true they made a fine start when as founder members of the League in 1888 they finished third behind Preston North End and Aston Villa and in 1893 won the Cup. But trouble was not far ahead. In 1906 they completed a disastrous season and were relegated to Division Two, where they remained until 1923 without much glory, far from it. They dropped into Division Three (North), winning only 9 of their 42 games. But within a few years the name of Wolves was headline news. Between 1932 and 1965 they were Champions three times, runners-up five times and twice Cup winners, a magnificent record.

One of the most amazing aspects of modern football is the regrettable way that some of the great clubs of the past have fallen from their pedestals. Clubs like Huddersfield Town, one of the most respected and popular teams of the twenties with their Championship hat-trick (1924, '25 and '26) following their Cup triumph in 1922. Then there are the two Sheffield clubs United and Wednesday, two of the "greats" both with Championship and Cup honours; Blackburn Rovers one of the first real giants of the game and Portsmouth, who dropped out of Division One in 1961, after winning the Cup and two Championships, and slid right down to Division Four.

History proves that it is much easier to drop out of the limelight that surrounds greatness than it is to climb back to the highest peaks, as so many clubs have discovered.

Published by IPC Magazines Ltd., King's Reach Tower, Stamford St., London SE1 9LS, England. Sole Agents for Australia & New Zealand: Gordon & Gotch Ltd.; South Africa: Central News Agency. Printed in England by Fleetway Printers, Gravesend, Kent. Covers laminated by Olro Coating Ltd. using Bexphane film. SBN 85037-580-0.

Twenty Question
QUIZ

1. Colin Lee (Chelsea), Alan Biley (Derby), Frank Worthington (Birmingham) and Eric Steele (Watford) were transferred during 1979-80. Their new clubs are in brackets. . . . can you name their former ones?

2. Terry Yorath (left) of Tottenham reached his 50th full cap for Wales when he skippered them against West Germany, Turkey or Belgium in a European Championship or World Cup game in November, 1979?

10. Which two clubs would be in opposition if the 1977 Scottish Premier Division Champions met the 1977 English F.A. Cup holders? CELTIC & MAN. UTD

11. During 1979-80, Sunderland's Mick Docherty was forced to retire due to injury. Can you name the two clubs he previously played for?

12. Queens Park Rangers' Clive Allen (below) had a sensational 1979-80 season when he scored over 20 goals. He is the son of Lee, Les or Len Allen? LES.

3. Aston Villa's Jimmy Rimmer (above) has played for three other League clubs. can you name them?

4. Mike Smith resigned as manager of Wales to take over as boss of which Football League club?

5. One of the biggest surprises of last season's League Cup was Swindon's fine 4-3 win against Arsenal in the Quarter-Finals. Did Alan Mayes, Chris Kamara or Andy Rowland score the winner in extra-time? ANDY ROWLAND.

6. Crystal Palace central defender Jim Cannon (left) is an under 21 international with which country? SCOTLAND.

7. Dundee United won their first- ever major trophy when they captured last season's League Cup by beating Aberdeen 1-0, 2-0, or 3-0 in a replayed Final? 3-0

8. Rearrange the jumbled letters to find the name of a top striker and his club. . .NNKYEGLLHDSIA (OOVRLP... EIL). KENNY DALGLISH. LIVERPOOL

9. Tony Woodcock was transferred from Nottingham Forest to which West German club? COLOGNE